Dark Psychology and Mind Control

Learn How to Awaken Emotional Intelligence within You, Practice Mind Hacking with Manipulation Techniques, Persuasion and Influence Even a Giant Mind

Anthony Secrets

Table of Contents

Introduction

The following chapters will discuss how to awaken your emotional intelligence within you. It will go ahead and provides various mind hacking techniques. The book focuses on the practice of these techniques. The art of persuasion is key even when encountered with a giant mind. The book focuses on the mastery of this art. It equips you with tools that will enable you to manipulate other people's minds to your advantage.

There are numerous books that focus on this particular topic. Thanks again for choosing to settle on this one. Every bit of it is carefully constructed in order to make sure that you get the maximum out of it, please enjoy!

Why Dark Psychology and Mind Control?

Dark psychology refers to the art of making others relate to what you want because of the way you express it to them. Manipulation is key. Various individuals employ this tactic in their day to day activities. Dark psychology refers to the science of mind manipulation. Psychology refers to the study of human behavior not limited to their thoughts, interactions and how they respond to various stimuli.

An introduction of the term dark changes the context of psychology into one that people employs techniques of manipulation, motivation, and persuasion in order to achieve the desired result. The book encompasses a wide view of dark psychology. After an interaction with this book, you will be able to achieve: effective mind manipulation, whether it actually works, the difference between brainwashing and mind control and how organizations use mind manipulation as a technique of coercion.

Chapter 1: The Power of Persuasion

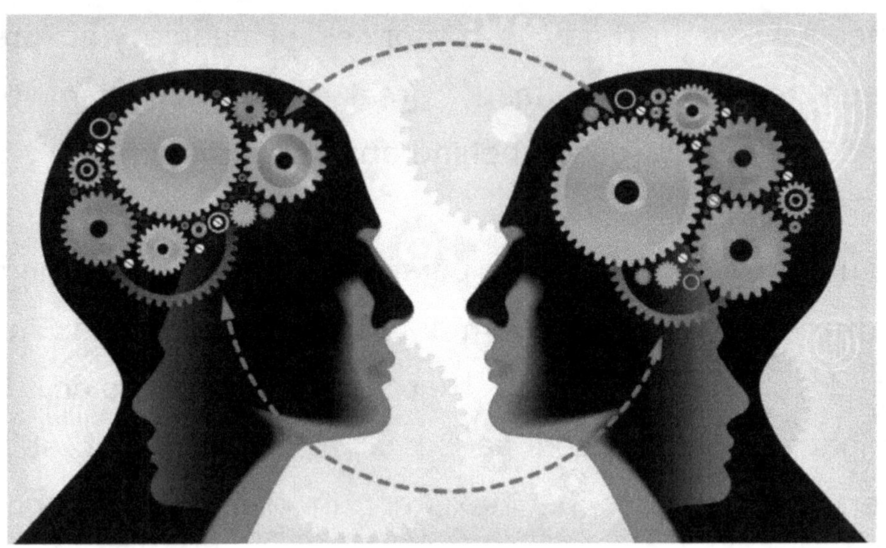

Persuasion refers to the act of addressing arguments to someone with the intention of selling them your school of thought pertaining to a particular subject matter. Persuasion also can be an argument or another statement that is intended to influence the other party. The ability of a person to influence another person's mind is their persuasiveness. This particular society that we live in today is comprised of people who are keen to know the neatly great ties. They want to understand the reason behind any phenomenon.

Thus they prefer being persuaded to do something rather than engaging them on a basis of command. The road to change is one that involves persuasion. It might be for a good cause or a bad one but still, persuasion has to be inexistent in order to influence change.

In order to participate actively in the art of persuasion, an individual needs a candid understanding of influential skills. With these skills in place, whatever you desire from another person will be easy to acquire. This is because you are in a position to be able to influence them to work in your advantage. An individual with good persuasion skills experiences;

clear paths that have minimal setbacks, heightened self-esteem because of the mastery of the art of interacting with other people. When it comes to communication, persuasion is a very crucial tool. For instance, persuasion techniques will be helpful to an employee, a customer or a salesperson. To a person whose day job is numerous interactions with other people, mastery of the art of influencing becomes a plus one to them. With effective persuasion techniques, employees may end up being promoted, an advocate is able to defend his or her stand a, and a businessman will able to secure his bid.

We often fail to understand why it is that some people can talk us into things that we did not want to engage in the first place. The degree of being persuaded depends on various factors. For instance, the state of emotions that you are in is a key yardstick when it comes to persuasion. When you crave for something, you are in a position that you can do almost everything and anything in order to make sure that you have it. This also relates to persuasion. In order to avoid falling victim of this technique, an individual needs to ensure that all his or her basic needs are taken care of. We all need to be careful when accepting gifts that satisfy our wants. The effect is usually short term but the result of this is long term. This means that you will always spend more time trying to pay back these individuals.

Basically, we need to appreciate the fact that if something touches our emotional quotient; it will always tend to pull you towards persuasion. This instance is almost unnoticeable. This is because we always tend to act on the heat of passion. An individual may be apt enough to think that he or she would not be swayed by the art of persuasion but as soon as the subject reaches the emotional quotient, your overall outlook with regards to it changes. You adopt a different perspective that is mitigatory in nature. Here you are working towards reaching an understanding but not maintaining your stand.

From our life experiences, we all have a story to tell on how persuasion has in the worst of scenarios made people engage in activities that do not reflect their personality but rather how easy they tend to be swayed. Below are pointers to effective persuasion:

Being Reciprocal

This refers to the proverbial adage of "scratch my back I scratch yours." As human beings, we are often inclined to buy the school of thought that many people are hostile. With this in place, we will be drawn to acts of good faith. This happens whenever an individual extends a kind gesture towards us. We will keep this in our long-term memory and often what reminds us of them will be this kind gesture. When you meet these individuals again, you would want to do the same and extend the same kind gesture that they showed to you in the first place. This will be regardless of whether they are in need or not. The same happens during persuasion. An individual may extend a kind gesture to you a first no matter how remote. If you do no notice this technique at this instance then you might be in for persuasion and you may realize this when it is too late. Once this gesture is at home with you, you will feel obliges to do the same. In most instances, people will always be inclined to assure the other party that they owe them a great deal. This becomes a win to the persuader. From this stage, it is you who will be on the giving end. You might realize that you made a mistake in assuring the other party of your support but this may be too late. You already have a feeling of guilt when you talk to the person.

The business world has embraced these tactics through the use of free samples. These are portions of the main product that are issued to those willing to buy for free. They are usually designed to make you have a feel of what you are buying. Many people will not comprehend this. After tasting or taking the free sample, this is when the obligation to buy rests with you solemnly. You will experience some level of guilt that will make you be obliged to purchase it even if it does not work for you.

 A good scenario, for instance, is the kind gesture that Mexico extended to Ethiopia when they were being invaded by Italy during the scramble and partition of Africa. Mexico offered diplomatic aid to Ethiopia and as a result, Ethiopia was not colonized. When the tragedy of the earthquake hit Mexico, Ethiopia had to retaliate and issue a reciprocal humanitarian even though the situation in Ethiopia was not rosy. It is common for individuals to do good things to us without necessarily wanting a reciprocal treatment. Despite this, it is key to note that the feeling of owing someone something is of great influencing value.

Internal Consistency

We are diverse beings of apt intellect. As human beings, we tend to buy from various schools of thoughts. Owing to this mere fact, we are often inclined to various preferences not limited to food, clothing and even various opinions with regards to different topics. People of high repute have always bought from different schools and when this is the case, they will always different their stand in one way or another. One way of denoting your stand is through writing and affirming about a particular opinion. For instance, when judges in a Court of law fail to reach a consensus and there is one of them or a number who have a different view, they are always inclined to draft a dissenting opinion whereby they explain the reasons as to why they do not buy from the other school of thought.

With this draft in place, you will be tied to your opinion henceforth. This means that any other matter arising with the same facts, you will treat them according to the way you had earlier denoted in the draft. This means that you are bound to follow suit with your future decisions to the latter. When we are of high repute, often we tend to show others that we are stern and firm when it comes to sticking by our word. Once you have a draft on a particular subject matter, you will be inclined one way or another to follow consistency.

When it comes to brainwashing, this does not relate to it in a literal context. Brainwashing refers to the act of making the brain devoid of the thoughts and beliefs it had earlier on and then feeding it with fresh beliefs. Take, for instance, you the American prisoners during the Korean war who were brainwashed by making them read anti-American beliefs in the manner of the first persona. This way they achieved brainwashing by first believing in what they were reciting.

Bullying has no different approach since you only engage in bullying after the original bully influences them to join through extending some kind gesture to the victim being bullied. Once this has been established, the act of bullying will switch its position in the mind of the first-timer. Bullying to him or she will seem so normal that the individual will start engaging in it repeatedly. Your self-image should be guarded with your heart. Once it changes, you will have to follow suit whether you like it or not. You will be obliged to feel consistent with your acts and this is what will destroy your self-image totally. You ought to realize that you stand for yourself and that your deeds are a reflection of who you are.

Social peer

As human beings, we are very observant to changes. We often stress ourselves with what is in fashion. Is something fashionable enough to put on to a particular event? Are you at par with a pa a particular social class? What will people say about me if participate in a particular deed? These are the questions that often cloud our mind in a bid to fit into society. Failing to fit in often takes a toll on various individuals to the extent that these individuals may live their whole lives in the shadows. To other people who feel that they have a point to prove, they will thrive with the change, embrace new cultures. All this in a bid to fit in the society. When this happens, the personality of an individual is completely lost. This now means that the individual will always be swayed by any happening.

Sometimes we do things out of our own liking but at times we want to prove a point to the crowds. Take for instance the onset of social media. There are a number of platforms that provide a solid base when it comes to communication. These can be said to be requisite. However, there are others that people join in order to be associated with a particular class of people.

Predetermined Perception

Growing up as children, we did not have a clear understanding as to what is good and what is not. We always followed the sayings of an adult. Owing to this, we were inclined to draw our basis from instructions. One would say for instance that, "dad said we should not go out of the compound." This is what stuck in our minds and provided a basis for everything you were not supposed to do. As adults, we have a clear understanding of the world and now we tend to draw our inferences from facts. There are various topics that experts in those fields have had a say about it. These topics usually form a building block towards our preferences. Nowadays, you are likely to meet arguments as the doctor said, the technician said, these are arguments that have a basis and are not just in actual floatation.

When responding to these perceptions, we tend to act according to what is said and not what we think as of right. It is normal to find a person who is sane acting in a manner that suggests differently. The problem arises where you realize that authority can easily be faked or misrepresented. When this happens, the party misrepresenting is the only one who is wary of that fact. The other party is acting solemnly of his or her previous perceptions of that authority. Thinking on our feet is something that should not be taken away from us. You ought to evaluate the consequences of an act before engaging in it headfirst lest we fall victims to persuasion.

The Degree of Liking

As human beings, we will be inclined to listen to the people whom we like. This is basic science. Our bodies will be attracted to the places where it does not face irritation. We all have an inherent factor that makes us either like or hate particular groups of people.

This is often dependent on our past experiences as human beings. We will hate a particular group of people just because a portion of them messed you up big time a while back. Take for instance the issue with patriarchy. Women are inclined to adopt a "men are dogs" approach owing to the historical mistakes of particular men in the past. When you have a liking towards a particular individual, you will be fixed to what they tell you. You will be inclined to believe them just because you like them. Likable people are perhaps the best persuaders because the mere fact of liking them overwhelms the brain to the extent that you have clouded judgment.

Moreover, when it comes to various issues in life, we express our attitude in discrepancy. Most of us will be inclined to shop where we are already known and that the customer service will be better than where we are not known. When a person is physically attractive, liking them becomes easy and in turn, this is what makes them the best persuaders. Most salesperson will be generally attractive as a business strategy to attract customers. The game is often played in a manner that the people you like the most will not always have the best intentions at heart.

Rarity

Making something rare increases its value. Take for instance during drought and famine, food has almost the same value as gold and gems. This might not be the case when there is plenty of food. When food is in abundance, people treat it as normality. This is not the case when food disappears. People will perform any kind of deed just to put food in their mouths. The same happens in persuasion. For instance, you will find a company issuing offers on the sale of some products at a cheaper price. In order for the company to enhance these products to be bought, they centralize the location of where these goods are found and then work on a deadline that works to their favor. Owing to this, people will hurry in order to acquire these goods while they still last.

In life, we go through a lot of experiences. Take for instance you have a parent that does not appreciate your progress whatsoever. They are the pushy type, the type that makes you work harder even if you are at your best. When these type of parents express some degree of happiness towards your progress, you will have a feeling of gratefulness towards them. The one-time happiness becomes of value to you than an individual who is always happy and cheerful around you. You will keep thriving to impress them over and over.

Chapter 2: Dark Psychology

Dark psychology refers to the art of studying human behavior in order to take advantage of the psychological nature of others. This often involves the tendency of people preying on others in order to achieve what they desire. Being equipped with the knowledge of dark psychology is almost advantageous as having superpowers can be. Psychology entails the understanding of how a human mind works. Often you will find that some people react to different situations with a discrepancy. This means that there might be triggers to a person's emotions that may not necessarily trigger to somebody else's emotion. The understanding of these two is what makes psychology interesting. Acquisition of knowledge is key because it is a very powerful tool. Having knowledge about something is almost as equivalent to having a weapon against something.

Psychology cuts across various fields not limited to religion, finance, crime and the choice of what and who to love and why. There are numerous psychological principles that come as a result of the mastery of human influence. Understanding the psychology of individuals often makes it easier to interact with them. Once you are able to interact with them, manipulating them becomes easier. When seeking to extract psychological information from an individual, this is going to be an uphill task because you are not going indirectly. You have to calculate your path as you maneuver step by step until you are able to reach his or her cognitive.

Just like a book, the human mind stores critical information in the very deepest parts of your conscience. This is what makes retrieving of this information subtle. In order to reach the deepest parts of the human mind, there are various triggers that are required in order to achieve this. You will often encounter information that is useless to you. The way you treat this information will determine how well you will fare on with your dark psychology.

In this world that we live in today, we experience dark psychology in almost every instance. We have to be wary of the facts that these numbers are rising and soon or later we are going to be victims of dark psychology. We have an option of accepting it, learning it and adopting protective measures in order to make sure that you and your loved ones are devoid of this mind manipulation and exploitation. The result of this is often being misused and taken for granted.

A comprehension of how this type of psychology works will see to it that you adopt defensive measures towards this type of phenomenon. In an attempt to go on with your life with much ease, there are techniques that will see to it that this happens. In a bid to distinguish who is a dark psychologist and who is not, there are various pointers that are key when working to reach this outcome. They include but are not limited to:

Narcissists

These are individuals who suffer from a certain kind of personality disorder. They often have an elevated sense of being in that they feel like they are on top of every other being. Their nature is characterized by bragging and looking down upon others. Mostly this kind of people will want things to go on the way they desire and a shift in the outcome of events has an effect on their emotions. A narcissist can also be referred to as a self-promoter because they see no good in others but only in themselves. This kind of people is often inclined to employ the effects of dark psychology in order to experience the outcome that they desire.

Machiavellians

This is high-level mind manipulators. They prey on the scarcity of instances that you are alert. If you have ever been conned, there is a period where you realize that you have lost a particular type of valuable and the chances of you getting it back are next to none. This is because it is already late and that you have no control of overturning the events. Machiavellians often have a higher sense of manipulating. The degree I higher than that of narcissists. Often this type of people would be involved in white-collar crimes. The ability of an individual to manipulate somebody of high repute and get away with it. They focus on these crimes because they are masters of intuition

Psychopaths

When it comes to psychopaths, the degree of manipulating has increased. Psychopaths extend to even cause physical harm to an individual's wellbeing. They act on impulse and are rowdy individuals who do not have a picture of what consequences are. Their lives are one that is full of thrill not knowing what may happen next. Crime is their way of life. However, these type of individuals involves violence in whatever they do. They will injure you physically just to get you out of their way. Their disorder is with the conscience since they have no feeling of remorse whatsoever. The degree of psychopathy varies from one individual to another. Research has it that there are a number of psychopaths whose degree of psychopathy is minimal to the extent that they stay out of crime.

Machiavellians, Psychopaths, and Narcissists are often the kind of people that are very good at creating first impressions. The first time you meet with them you will be inclined to think otherwise. The longer you stay with them is when you get to know how ill-mannered they can be. When it comes to certain instances in life, these particular individuals tend to perform better than others because of their ability to relax under pressure, the lack of anxiety and the way they can express themselves properly without fear of masses. These people have an elevated sense of proving that they are better than others and this is what makes them a nuisance. When it comes to job scavenging, these skills are very crucial.

Sadists

These are individuals who are inclined to find peace in the worst of events. They are the type of people who enjoy when others suffer. They have an effect of not being at peace when somebody else is enjoying. Often they exhibit cruelty towards others and this is what makes them sadists. These kind of people are not manipulative or impulsive in the way they do things. With these types of traits in place, sadists have been found to be drawn to jobs that are in the same kind of nature as their personality. These type of people will often opt for jobs such as The Police or The military. These jobs have a justification of harming others and this is what they thrive for.

How Dark Psychology Works

In order for us to gather what dark psychology refers to, we first need an understanding of what the dark side of a person refers to. From the face value of it, it is safe to say that the dark side of an individual is the individual's worst behaviors when not monitored. The dark side of a person is what the individual turns to when faced with tragedy.

The dark side of an individual is often in relation to the most aggressive and anti-social instincts that make us not be appreciated by others because of the way we treat them. Acting in impulsion is what makes most people dark. Most people picture their darkest fantasies as being the worst of scenarios. This might not be the case as you may find out that your dark side is not as demonic as you had thought.

Among the many attributes of dark side psychology, there is the aspect of undetected mind control. This type of mind control is the most dreaded. It is normal to know when someone is controlling you mentally because you can easily put a stop to it. You can take measures that will enable you to stay void of the controlling. This may include even staying away physically just to make sure you do not encounter the person. However, when you are of the mind-controlling individual, then it will eat you up from the inside like a fire trying to consume you. Picture this instance where somebody is robbing from you yet you are not aware. The behavior will continue until it reaches a point whereby there is nothing more to rob thus leaving you void. You are not able to take up defenses to this particular type of manipulation until it is too late.

When it comes to mind control there are two techniques that an individual may use in order to make sure that your mind is under attack completely.

Interactions among people and the use of media are crucial when it comes to manipulating others. In the past, the media was a channel that was only available to large corporations that could afford it. For individuals, their only mind-controlling technique was through interacting with people at personal levels. With the advent of technology, the media is at the disposal of anyone and thus mind manipulation has advanced a notch higher.

Hypnotism

During the whole process of mind manipulation, the other party employs hypnotism. Hypnotism refers to the state which the human mind is focused on a particular thing. With this type of focus in place, there will be reduced peripheral knowhow. Peripheral know-how refers to the act of not knowing what is happening around an individual surrounding due to the fact that you have fully focused your attention on what is being said. Absence of peripheral awareness is what makes this particular type of people to thrive. The human mind will be focused on providing a suggestion that was already calculated by the other party. This, in turn, has the ultimatum of making the person think that the suggestion was solely born by him.

There are theories that tend to explain what goes on in the mind during hypnosis. The first theory known as the Altered State of mind theory is to the effect that hypnosis is a state of mind that is a theory that visualizes hypnosis as an altered state of mind. This altered state of mind is represented by a higher level of know-how that is elevated as compared to consciousness. The second theory visualizes hypnosis as the imagination of yourself in the role desired. This is known as the non-state theory.

There are a number of things that one experiences during hypnosis. First is that the mind is in a state of elevated concentration and focus. During this concentration, the person focuses on that specific memory of thought shielding all the other thoughts from distracting it. If you want to know that a subject is hypnotized, you will find that you are in a position to offer more suggestions in relation to that topic. The whole process of making you a hypnotized follows a process known as induction. There are different forms of hypnosis some are medically induced while others are in the form of stage performance or art. You should be keen enough to know when you are being induced to hypnotization.

Deception

What follows hypnotization is deception. Deception takes many forms. It can range from complete lie to several omissions in the truth. Deception may include anything not limited to propaganda, distraction and even concealment that are made in mala fide in order to make you buy a school of thought that is misconceived. When in a relationship, you are often inclined to trust what your partner is discharging to you. Since the building blocks to a good relationship is often dependent on trust. As an individual in a relationship, you will expect that at all times you will be told the truth. People who have adapted to lies and misconceptions are often inclined to think that everyone will react in the same way as the person who first misconceived them. They are in anticipation that they might be lied to again. Such kind of people have issues believing in what other people say. We should be keen to remember that deceit assumes various hats and that it can be used to fraudulently misrepresent you. The best thing is that the courts have counter-measure towards this kind of issues.

Brainwashing

Apart from deceit, there comes in a phenomenon known as brainwashing. Brainwashing has been given many terms that can be used to refer to it. Many people call it re-education or even though reform and control. From the wording of it, one can deduce that brainwashing is the process by which your previous beliefs towards a particular phenomenon are removed and replaced with the desired ones. Brainwashing is said to have an effect in reducing how the individual thinks without external influence. This way the mind will be dependent on the introduction of novel thoughts that will be of influence to his feelings, attitude, and lifestyle.

Brainwashing has its roots from China. It was then capitalized upon by attorneys in Germany. It went further to set its roots in the United States as a platform for trafficking in human beings. In the precolonial period, this concept was used when introducing colonialist to different religious quotients.

Before an individual engages in something, there has to be an inspiration that makes them move. There has to be a drive that pushes them forward. With mind manipulation, there is no difference to it. There is a range of inspiration that makes people turn sour and start engaging in these mind games. The major inspiration will be that you want a person to behave in a manner that is advantageous or purposeful to you. When manipulation fails to hit the base, the other party may be inclined to adopt a new method that involves playing with the mind. Thus mind games

Techniques Used to Achieve Dark Psychology

In order to achieve dark psychology, there are a number of techniques that might come in handy. Normal getting the attention of others in order to convey a particular message is usually the hardest part.

Using Even if the technique

As human beings, we are born equally, with equal opportunities that will savor all of us. This is not the case as many of us tend to think that we are above others. We are obliged not to settle for less and rather for more. Typically when you are conversing with someone maybe on a particular subject matter, the individual will tend to act in a manner that they are of a high profile and thus they require the best. Take for instance when a business person is selling property, the ultimate aim he or she has is that the property should be disposed of no matter what happens. When the potential buyer sites that the product may not be right for them, the even if strategy comes in. You are aiming to show this person that the product will still be of use to them and that they should buy it. This is, in turn, advantageous to you.

Anticipation

Anticipation is key during persuasion. This is because anticipation brings about anxiety that is overrated. Take for instance you are offered goods now and after week. The difference between these two goods is that you are going to pay higher for the goods that are to be delivered the same day as opposed to paying for the goods that are to be delivered after one week. People have time and again exhibited the behavior that they do not wish to procrastinate. You would rather pay more and be assured of goods the same day than wait for a whole week for the goods you would have acquired the same day.

Excitement plays an important role when it comes to this kind of individuals. One may be overwhelmed about the occurrence of a particular event to the extent that it brings about restlessness. This individual is not able to function properly because of the mere fact that they are anticipating a particular occurrence. When persuading an individual using anticipation, you ought to first build the excitement. Cultivate the excitement to a level that you know the person being persuaded is craving for the goods. At this point, then go ahead and use anticipation as your tool.

Analogical Reasoning

When you are presenting your idea to an audience, it is important to take note that they should be able to comprehend and digest it in a manner that will be of merit to you. A shoddy explanation would not work when you are encountering gigantic minds. Another way of making sure that the audience is actively elating to your topic is through giving it a basis from a phenomenon that people have understood in the past. This will make the topic easy to digest. Reasoning from this particular point of view gives you an upper hand when you are dealing with gigantic minds. This lowers their levels of thinking to yours. Once this happens, you are able to relate to them one on one.

Our minds have an effect of relating everything it processes to pictures in order to digest and decode the information properly. Take for instance you are explaining to the audience your idea about lighting and you are taking them back to the rainbow. The rainbow is as basic as it is. This will create an impression in the mind of the audience about the lighting that you are talking about.

Curiosity

The void that rests between what we know and what we do not know is what brings about curiosity to us as human beings. Knowledge is power, what you know might affect you in ways that you do not even comprehend. There are a number of things that bring about curiosity. This curiosity is an important aspect to play with because it will always draw the audience's attention towards you.

Take for instance a series of events left unfinished will bring about curiosity. When people have different expectations as to what is happening, this will also bring about curiosity. When someone else has information that we do not, we tend to be curious. In order to master this art, one needs to understand how to play around with these aspects'

Chapter 3: Dark Psychology Applied in Seduction (Practical Examples Applied to Seduction)

Seduction is an art in life that can either bring people pain or pleasure, and anyone can master it. Dark psychology can not only be applied in seduction but also in commercials, sales techniques, internet ads, and even in business. As a parent, you will also find them mostly in your teenagers as they try to get what they want. Dark psychology works where there are trust and love. Below are some of the dark psychology methods applied in seduction;

1. Superficial Charm

Superficial charm is also known as a glib charm or insincere charm. A manipulator tends to be engaging, smooth, and slick. This type of manipulation is most common in a narcissist. Narcissists are manipulative and entrap their victims via They will use their charming ways to make you fall in love with them to satisfy their need. They will never reciprocate their feelings in any way. People with such traits are narrow-minded and often portray an impression of a well-mannered person. They are irresistibly charming, especially to the opposite sex. By use of superficial charm, a man will often go out of his way to please the woman and will always get what he wants.

2. Flattery

Flattery is also known as blandishment or adulation. It is the act of giving compliments in excess and for self-centered reasons. These compliments are mostly insincere or farfetched truths. Flattery is also the use of sweet words in an attempt to get sexual relationships. A manipulator will successfully hide their true intent by use of an appeal to flattery. They will also manage to weaken their prey's judgment as flattery will offer a distraction. The prey or audience will be subjected to flattery only if they will comply with the manipulator. Flattery is a smooth form of seduction as women love compliments, and it is always a sure way to start a conversation. Every woman wants to know that she looks good and feel appreciated, and it is difficult to differentiate a good compliment and flattery as only a very thin line separates them. Philosophers and historian have pointed out flattery as a problem in ethics and politics.

Here are some ways that flatterers scheme to consume you in;

- The flatterers use praise as a calculated move to get in your good books. They will always go out of their way to support your point of view and win your favor.

- They will always butter up the victim first before proposing a deal that will most likely benefit them more than you. They will make you feel more special, intelligent, and superior to achieve their goal.
- The unethical ones will even give you fake praises and dupe you to disclosing highly sensitive information about you and then shamelessly use it against you.

3. Love Bombing

It is no longer a secret that too much of something is poisonous, either in the positivity or negativity of it. Love as well should have a constant measure, not too little and not too much. Love bombing is an effort to influence a person by use of attention and attraction. Abusive narcissists always try to use it to gain a victim's confidence. One major sign of love bombing at the beginning of a relationship is a lot of attention in a short period and immense pressure for speedy commitment. It is usually the first sign, and if a narcissist is successful, he can easily control his prey.

The love bombing phases are idealization, devaluation, and discard.

- Idealization

This defense mechanism is when an individual views all people as good. In this mechanism, the individual attributes optimistic qualities to self and others.

- Devaluation

This mechanism is the opposite of idealization. Unlike idealization, devaluation is whereby an individual attributes negative qualities to self or other people.

- Discard

An abuser who has successfully entrapped you and taken you through the above two processes will eventually discard you but not for long as they will always crawl back to repeat the process over and over again and with each cycle, you die a little inside.

To break off from an abuser's web or better still to avoid being trapped in the web, psychologist advises us to be observant; to always look and listen. It is also advisable to seek family support as well as friend's support.

4. Reverse Psychology

This technique involves asserting a behavior or belief opposite from the one desired. By applying the above technique, a person expects that the subject will be encouraged or persuaded to do what is desirable. A manipulator will always come up with an option and make it fixed on people's mind. He will use all means possible, including verbal cues to make it enticing. He will then argue against the option he wants and then finally push them to make a final decision. When you approach a woman, she automatically assumes that you are interested in her, and she even becomes sure of it when you try so hard to impress her. In reverse psychology, a man gives attention to other people, and in return, the woman will always work hard to grab his attention.

5. Fractionation

Fractionation is a hypnosis tactic that makes women get to a mix of emotions and fix all of their ecstasies to you. A woman subjected to this type of hypnosis will emotionally depend on the man wholly and agree to every of his demand. Fractionations is more like short-circuiting a woman's brain and make her fall in love with you in the shortest time possible. In fractionation, you make a bond with the desired woman then break it; you then pull her back and make a second bond which is always stronger than the previous one. Fractionation is more like walking on thin ice. If used wrongly, it can cause irreversible damage to a woman's psyche. Fractionation works on any woman. It can make a woman fall in love with you faster than the magic money and wealth performs on a woman. Nevertheless, if used correctly, it is the best method to seduce a woman.

6. Gaslighting

Gaslighting technique makes a woman question her sanity. You sow seeds of doubt on a target and make her question her memory. Narcissists and sociopaths always use this method on their victims and manage to abuse them. A man who wants full control of a woman's feelings and actions will always prefer this method. So, what are the signs of gaslighting?

- Verbal abuse but dressed up as a joke.
- It is downplaying the importance of an emotion or action.
- It is undermining the worth of the victim.
- Diverting and to some extent blocking a victim's attention to the outside world.

The seed of doubt sown in gaslighting and lack of people in the outside world to confide in, a woman will be like a puppet on a man's hand and can be manipulated easily. There are three common methods used in gaslighting;

a) **Hide:** A man may hide things from a woman and cover up the action. In a normal circumstance, the man should feel ashamed, but in gaslighting, he convinces a woman to doubt her own belief, and in the end, she blames herself.

b) **Change:** The man will feel the need to change the woman's act or dressing code and mold them to the woman of their fantasy. If the woman does not obey, she is made to believe that she is not good enough.

c) **Control:** The man seeks full control of the woman without regards to her feelings or emotions. He has no regard for what the woman wants or thinks. To achieve this, he secludes the woman from family and friends, and it gives the man pleasure.

7. Pigeonholing

A man will use this method to make a woman do what he wants her to do or not do what he doesn't want her to do. It is a method of making a woman think that she is creepy. You do that by stopping her from doing some things and claiming they are weird. You might as well ask her if she is. By doing that you will make her avoid doing that specific act so as not to be labeled weird. Her insecurities will do the magic for you, and there is an assurance that she will never repeat that.

This tactic is a sure bet as women like a domineering and authoritative man. If the man tried to dominate her directly, the feminist in her would awake, and she would rebel, but through pigeonholing, the man dominates over her subconsciously. The female mind has a flow as it makes decisions emotionally unlike its male counterpart, which makes its decisions rationally.

8. Extreme Verbal Abuse

This technique is not for the faint-hearted. It is a recovery method. A good example is if you are in a relationship and just out of nowhere, the woman suddenly shuts you out. You try all methods to reach her, but she completely ignores you. So, what do you do? You send a one-word text with an obscene word and let her do the magic from there. Women will tend to get mad, and in that, you will get a reaction from her, after all, any reaction despite being negative is better than no reaction. In that situation, when she replies, you should revert to your normal self and act as if nothing happened. This method has high chances of recovery, and her interests in you will be improved.

9. Brainwashing

Brainwashing, also known as mind control is the concept of altering or controlling the human mind using some psychological techniques. A man who wants to control a woman will often use brainwashing to have the upper hand in that relationship. A manipulator will often use different brainwashing techniques, and these are the most common techniques to look out for;

- Isolation- A man isolates the woman from family and friends. By doing this, he is sure that the woman has no one to confide in other than him. The woman will only get information and ideas from the man, and he comfortably gives her only what he wants her to know. By doing this, he is sure that there will be no third party involved to question his ideas and decisions.

- Attack on self-esteem- After isolating the woman, you have to break her and rebuild her in the man's desire. The attacks are made in the form of ridicule or by intimidation. The man has to make sure that he has a superior position for this to be successful.
- Mental abuse- Mental torture is a worse form of torture even than physical torture. In this technique, the man will embarrass the woman in front of others with the truth. He can also not give the woman any personal space and keep badgering her.
- Allowing contact only with brainwashed members: Peer pressure is highly influential. By allowing contact with only other brainwashed people, the woman will follow what the other people are saying with an attempt to wanting to be liked and accepted.

10. Psychological Manipulation

Psychological manipulation is a social influence that targets to alter the behavior of others through deception or abusive attacks. What methods can a man use to control a woman?

- Positive Reinforcement: He can use praises, excessive apologizing, money, gifts, and facial expressions like a smile or even public recognition.
- Negative Reinforcement: The perfect examples to achieve this are via nagging, yelling, silent treatment, crying, threats, swearing, emotional blackmail, and playing the victim among many others.
- It encourages the woman to keep on trying to make the relationship work, but at the back of the man's mind, he knows that failure lies ahead.
- Lying by Omission: A man withholds a trivial amount of truth. It can also be known as propaganda.
- Denial: The man adamantly denies that he has done something wrong.
- Guilt Tripping: This is an intimidation tactic where the man insinuates that the woman does not care enough and that she is selfish. It makes the woman have self-doubt and makes her submissive always.

- Playing the Victim: The man will portray himself as the victim to gain pity and compassion from the woman. The woman will not stand to see him suffer, and she will easily cooperate.

- Shaming: The man uses sarcasm to instill fear on the woman. Shaming will make the woman feel unworthy. It can be via an obnoxious look, rhetorical comments or even a stern look.

11. Sycophancy

Sycophancy is a type of flattery but in an obedient manner. It is a successfully tested art that is highly fashionable. A sycophant is a very intelligent person with high grasping power and with an ability to read a person's mind. A sycophant smartly manipulates an individual to achieve his goals and dreams. The three scopes of sycophancy:

1. Obsequious flatter and servility

2. False accusation and tale-bearing

3. The character or characteristics of a sycophant

With the same breath, we should note the types of psychological manipulation of sycophancy. They are:

- Positive Reinforcement: They include flattery, giving money and gifts, giving praise, grooming, attention, seduction, smiling, and superficial sympathy.

- Negative Reinforcement: They include crying, emotional blackmail, anger, threats, victim-blaming, swearing, character assassination, nagging, to mention a few.

- Other Techniques: Diversion, deception, denial, exaggeration, lying, advertising, confidence trick, mind control, scapegoating, propaganda, rationalizing abuse, etc.

There is a thin line between loyalty and sycophancy as people stopped meaning what they say and saying what they mean. In the current world, words and thoughts no longer signify reality. In a sycophantic culture, people seek favor through flattering people with wealth and great influence. Sycophants never correct or criticize people in power, but they are always careful and too pleasant.

A sycophant will always agree with your thoughts or ideas regardless of whether they are good or bad. They never practice constructive criticism. Women are easily drawn by men who worship them and sing to their tune. They might think it is loyalty and love, but the line between the two and sycophancy is very thin. So, how do you recognize a sycophant?

a) They imitate your opinion, taste and looks too absurd lengths.

b) They are fashion stockers.

c) Always disagree on small issues to show that they have a mind of their own but always agree on big issues.

d) Always encourage one's worst tendencies and give support to and encourage them.

Sycophants are people-pleasers and are always quick to judge anyone who dares to judge the group-think or dare the leader. A healthy relationship needs a person of bravery who is willing to offer a different opinion from the consensus even if that jeopardizes the relationship. With different opinions expressed, there is a challenging seduction phase and a healthy relationship.

Chapter 4: Dark Psychology Applied in Business and Work

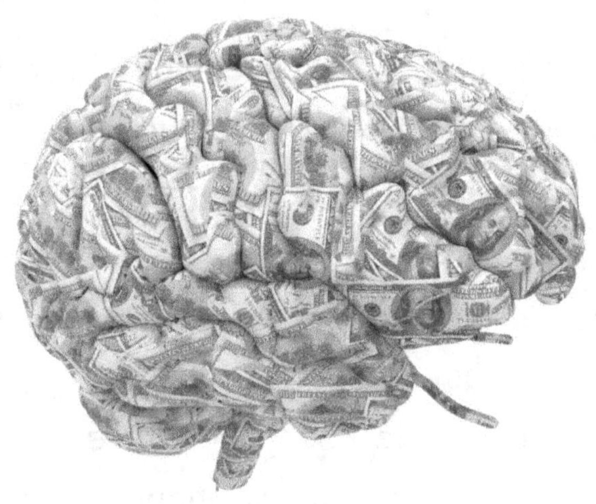

Dark psychology has been widely used by the superior to achieve success. The most successful businessmen normally use the dark triad to influence and exploit others to believe in what they do and to support their ideas in the business game. They use persuasive techniques to convince others to do the opposite of what they really wanted. The same tactics are used by businessmen to lure others into investing in their businesses.

Some people use dark psychology unknowingly and some fall into the risk of it being used against them when they don't realize it. Businessmen use this art to influence people and to convince them that what they are doing is right to earn them more trust in the market. Dark psychology in today's world is the most influencing technique used by people to achieve their goals and gain fame. In this chapter, we are going to learn more about the dark psychology applied in business and work.

Just like in other fields, it is helpful to apply dark psychology in business, to influence people for the success of your business. It may be not as easy as it sounds when you read about it in books and articles, but when you train your mind right, to understand and control your own emotions, then you can easily apply dark psychology in your business and attract the success you've been long yawning for. When you learn deep into psychology and learn the techniques of the dark triad, reading through other people's mind won't sound like a task to you anymore. You will have the opportunity to make Machiavellianism your own cup of tea to arrive at your desired destination.

As a business person, be the kind that can easily learn the emotions of those around you so that you have an easy time persuading them to like your business without necessarily making them feel pushed into to it. Have an influencing power as strong as that of politicians that will lead them to like your business willingly even if it was not exactly what they wanted. Try to make your products sound like the best in the market that everyone would like to get for themselves.

In any business there's always competition in the market and for you to market your products successfully you need both social and psychological skills that will help you understand your clients and convince them to purchase your products. The services you deliver to your clients are never regarded quality until you prove to them how quality they are, but how can you do this without having the power to convince and manipulate.

Businessmen all over the world attract public attention with their striking success. The light of their achievements leaves other people thinking hard on what they can do to score their best in the business sector. They keep wondering how these people manage to be successful within a short period of time unlike them who have to struggle and try here and there to get what best suits them and that they can easily manage until success is achieved.

Some employees to have started developing the tactics of the dark triad to influence their employers to get too attached to them for how they work. These employers have become masters of dark psychology that they can easily brainwash their bosses and coworkers that they all believe these people are perfectly fit in their positions and that the can deliver extraordinary services to the company.

Many employees have never understood why they can easily get fired while others will always remain to serve in the same position or even get promoted to higher positions. It is because of the techniques that these people have learned that enable them to work and get along with all kind of traits in people around them. They develop good social skills that allow them to interact with their employers and coworkers without crashing anyone's back.

People who are antisocial also use dark psychology as a weapon to prosper. They become too Machiavellian that no one finds they fault in anything they do. They use this trait to exploit everyone turning everything in their favor. They show shining success at the expense of other people. This is because they have indoctrinated everyone to always see the best in them.

Sociopaths are usually unemotional and too remorse so they use the dark personality to take advantage over others. When they are employees, they get their employers being too attached to them and believing in them more than they deserve. This gives them the opportunity to work on good terms with employers for a long time. They are trusted for who they are not and their experience in dark psychology allows them to hide under these traits without raising eyebrows.

If you ever wondered why many people are always successful and admire the lifestyle wishing you could be like them, then by the time you finish reading this book you would have understood everything to do with the dark psychology and how you can apply it in business and at work. Here we will learn about the practical exercises of dark psychology such as exaggeration, lying, Machiavellianism, silent treatment, emotional intelligence and many more that will be useful to you in your business while starting as a toddler and even after you have become PRO in the market.

The technique of exaggeration is the most commonly used by businessmen to market their products successfully. They want to praise their products so much to make you think more about their benefits over other products. They make you see only the good side of these products that you even forget to think about the side effects. When you pay attention to how they talk about the products they are selling you to you, you get so carried away and feel the urge to purchasing all of them.

Online marketers use ads to advertise their products on different social platforms. Some ads carry short video clips that explain the benefits of their products. The clips are always too much exaggerated to make you feel the importance of using the products. The benefits of it expressed in the clips make you so obsessed with it to an extent that you are persuaded to have a test of it personally.

The same way these adverts make you feel about the products you are looking for is how you should manipulate your customers to liking your products and always willing to promote your business. This will make your business glowing successful giving you the confidence to keep moving. Make others feel like your business is the best in the market and that they should not think of something else apart from your products.

Also, read through the mind of the people to learn what they like and what they don't. This will give you an easy task when selecting the products to market to them.

Most successful businesses are as a result of lies. In order to seek fame for their products, some businessmen have to lie about their products and what they can do. They deceive others to believe that their products are the best and that other similar products have side effects. They use lies to influence others to follow them and ignore other companies that produce similar products. They end up winning a large market as people are pushed to try their products and to add on, some people go as far as sharing about these products and their benefits over other similar products with friends and colleagues. When these people trust their friends, they will also want to have a try of what their friends have experienced giving the owner of the business a large market.

The tactic of lying also applies to work. You will find a worker lying about their job experience to get employed. They even get promoted to higher levels as many employers prefer giving high positions to experienced personnel so that they have their businesses managed the best way because they also want to be successful and they are not ready to be dragged behind.

To conduct your business in order, you will have to use the dark techniques to achieve what you desire. You can never be successful in a business when you openly talk about the side effects of your products to your target market. You must learn to avoid the negative side of it and use the positive side to influence people to like your products.

The same applies to work when you have to build a relationship with your employer, employee or coworker. You must make these people believe in your experience and what you can achieve in order to brainwash them to invest their trust in you even before you actually show them your potential.

To help your business thrive, always motivate others to believe in whatever you are doing and see it as the best. Use this trait to exploit their minds to follow your interest. This has helped many people to succeed with their business without necessarily having to beg people into supporting them. They are of great influence to those who see them prosper in the field of business.

Those who read and watch their success stories are highly driven to follow their steps to prosper as well. Their minds are restricted to believing that these people are intelligent and that by listening to them and following their moves, they will turn out as successful as them.

The silent treatment is one of the dark techniques usually used by employers to win their worker's mind. When something is done in a way that they don't consider right, they at times decide to go silent for quite long. Their silence attracts the workers' attention because they are left thinking of what went wrong and how they can make it right.

While they are thinking about what the matter is, they are manipulated to following the employer closely to find out what they really need to be done and how they can do it. The employer on the other side is benefiting as their interests are considered and are served right and according to their expectations.

To have your business shining with striking success, you need to learn how to deal with other people's emotions. Thoroughly read into their mind to understand how they feel and what they want. This will help you in coming up with the right products for them based on their interests. Designing products according to the interests of your clients earn you more market as never before.

The most successful people in the world always try to make other people think that there are the most intelligent. They use the power of their blooming success to exploit other people. They make others want to follow their steps because they believe this is the only way to success. Some people become more obsessed with them that they keep talking about them all the time telling others about the achievements of these millionaires.

These successful people have learned the social psychology of controlling other people's mind to gain more trust and confidence. They are always bold about how they carry out themselves and ready to make others believe that their ways of handling things are the best. They always want everything to run in their favor.

This technique is also used by leaders in workplaces to achieve great support from their team. Leaders who are great psychologists usually use dark triad to take advantage of others. They study the emotions of their teams and attempt to manipulate them to do things that only benefit their interests as a leader.

At work, whether you are an employer or a worker, you must always influence others to believe that you are the best service provider and that you don't need to follow-ups to work well. Dark tactics help you create a good relationship with people around you in workplaces without letting them notice that they are falling victims of manipulation.

When people like what you do, they will always be ready to offer their support to you. When they help you achieve your goals, you will be left thinking of what to offer them in return. Take your time to think about how you can reward them back. However, remember to keep your priorities untouched. What you are going to offer them must not interfere with your interests.

Getting your supporters something in return is okay, but doing this with at most intelligence is the most important. Focus on manipulating them to keep serving your interests and ensure that your missions are achieved through these people.

Whenever you are using dark psychology to pop out, never forget to be consistent in what you do or say. Remember here you are to be of influence to others. You are supposed to persuade them to choose your ideas over theirs, so when you keep changing from one thing to another your ideas will be pointless. You will fail in your mission of winning other people's trust when you don't stick to one idea.

You should not let these people know that you are trying to convince then to doing something that will only serve your interests at their expense. Keep focusing on one idea and make the rest of the team believe in the end results of the ideas you are bringing to them so that you find their full support.

To prosper in the business world, always love what you do and what others do as well. When you are a business person, the first fall in love with your business and treat it with a lot of passion then let your clients know that you like their ideas and interests. You may not necessarily love the ideas but to win clients, act like you love everything they say and also give them alternative suggestions and convince them to go for your idea with the mentality that they have made the right choice.

When you are an employer, show your workers that you like what they are doing and that their ideas are brilliant. If you have something that you would like to be done in a different way from how they are doing it, share out your ideas with them and convince them to consider your idea over their own.

Your business can only be successful when you have a good working relationship with your workers. They will respect your decisions when you respect their ideas and as a psychologist, you can always go for dark techniques to help you come out of the trap of serving the interests of others over your own.

Those in power are usually respected and many people believe that they are always right. They are very influential and they were ever admired by those who stalk them. They easily exploit people to do what they have an interest in and what they believe is the best.

When you want to market your business and have many people purchase your products, you can always take persons that are holding high and respected seats and are using these products to perform the advertisement of these products for you. Their stalkers will easily believe them more than when you just used an ordinary person to do the advertisement for you.

Their influence in others is so high and this will earn you more customers, gain your business fame and lead you smoothly towards turning out successful.

When letting people decide how you should offer services to them, always use the limited choices tactic. The options they have should be restricted to not including what they want to be done. Try as much as possible to give them options that will still lead them to what you want. By doing so, you will have them manipulated them to support your decisions.

This technique of dark psychology has helped many to reach their goals and it is of much importance in business and at work. You should know how to influence others to achieve a striking success.

The dark psychology when well learned and put into practice, you can easily reach your desired goal before you notice it. Even though some people unknowingly use these tactics to succeed, those who have learned emotional intelligence take advantage of their knowledge to brainwash others for their own benefit and in most occasions they succeed and become prosperous in their lives.

Politicians have used these tactics and we've seen them succeed and get votes. They have influenced others to believe that they are the most intelligent and the right people to lead the society. Not a small but a huge number of people have believed in them and offered them support.

Attorneys too have taken advantage of their knowledge in psychology to influence other people's mind to get what they want. They have succeeded in this and have rulings done in their favor. This has made them feel so within and important than other people and they are even respected for the sense of their psychology.

In business too, you can use dark psychology to manipulate people to like your products. You can learn them and understand what they like to help you in coming up with what best suits them. You need to get the best market to sell your products and achieve your purpose and this cannot be done when you just sit like any other normal person and wait for the business to take care of itself and meet its purpose.

 Dark psychology has been talked about as a threat to other people's state of life because they are not given the freedom to follow their own desires. However, when it comes to business and work, dark traits play a bigger role in achieving success. You have to get ahead of others and persuade them to get yourself a good market.

Chapter 5: How to Control the Mind without the Interlocutor Knowing

The main aim to control the thoughts of the person you are interacting with is to achieve your desired intention. You will get many things if you can take control of the other person mind. The approach and the techniques to use will determine whether you will be successful in achieving your goal. You need to get hold of their unconscious to influence them. Train to be a master in controlling ad at times manipulating your partner's mind and thoughts. It is attainable to take control of the intention of someone. You need to apply some techniques, and you will succeed. Some of the tricks to use for you to control your interlocutor's include;

Pay Attention

Pay attention to your interlocutor, and they will have the confidence to express what they feel. That will make them outpour their heart to you, and you will have a base to get control of their mind in any direction that you want. When you get them to trust you, they will not keep anything away from you. You will have the entire picture of everything, and you will know how to approach them. Make sure you talk about what makes them happy and what seems to interest them. If you get into a topic and you may not be conversant about the issue, ask questions as a way to show that you are interested. Showing that the talk is interesting to you will earn you more trust. You should tolerate them even if the conversation is boring. That way, you will be in a position to control their minds. Being attentive is a way of showing friendliness, and that will mean pleasant conversation. Talk to them as if you are seeking advice from a friend as well as an experienced person. Complimenting them will help you win their sympathy. Paying attention is a way to make someone think that you respect them. They too feel that you recognize them and trying to gently give your point of view will provide you with access to their mind and thoughts. Make them believe that you trust their ideas. If your interlocutor seems to be smarter than you, decide to play it cool and you will eventually succeed. In case of a dispute, do not shout them down but instead be polite and remain friendly. If that dispute is not of any importance, and they are proving hard to convince, find a wise way to end the conflict without offending them. Search a common ground if you want to persuade them and be sure that it is something that they will agree. Show how much you have in common, and that will make them friendly. Your attitude towards them matters a lot and will force them to compromise.

Demonstrate how their cooperation will be profitable and of convenience.

Hypnotism

It is a great approach to take control of someone's mind when to use in the right way. When used correctly, it will help you put your interlocutor in a trance within the first few minutes of your conversation. It is a way of seducing them, and you will get them to act your suggestions. They will not know that you are using your abilities to make them follow their ideas. Make sure they are flexible, and they have relaxed. When someone is relaxed, they put their guard down, and that will be an excellent opportunity to influence them in any way. Make them keep off many questions about any issue and you. Hence, you will increase your ability to exercise your influence. When you influence a conscious mind, it becomes easy to control the brain as well. Suggest what exactly you want them to do. Make the suggestion clear as well as compelling to influence their minds actively. When you use this approach correctly, you end up being a master in persuading people.

Control the Guard

To make any progress in mind-controlling, you need to suppress the brain shield. It is the conscious mind that you need to deal with in the first place. Use softer as well as subtle techniques to make sure that your interlocutor has relaxed. Try and get them to be in your debt, and this will prove influential. It is okay if you give your interlocutor favors moments before to make it simpler to control them. Doing them good from time to time will make them feel an obligation to do good in return. Doing all this will give you a better position in the way you relate. It is advantageous to do this regularly, and it will raise the perception of superiority. The superiority will allow you to access more things that are in the interlocutor's mind. You will have more power since the feeling of guilt in the other person mind will turn them to your will quickly.

Be Good to Them

Playing with a person's imagination is a fine art to controlling the mind. Use imaginations to change the other person's reality and make what you want to happen. Convince them that if a particular thing does not occur at the moment, it will be next to impossible to happen later. Be kind and offer multiple choices for them. There being overwhelming choices, their imagination will persuade them to try nearly all of them. Try and show them that following your idea would be the best thing for them to do. That will make them do what you want, and that will be an assurance that you already have control over their mind. Let what they imagine take over to leading them to see how your suggestion is powerful. Use imagination to find the best that you can acquire from a person.

Repeat Something Over and Over Again

Repeating something many times makes it sturdy, and that means that what we perceive is what we believe to be real. If you happen something severally, your interlocutor's mind will register that as being the real thing. Repetition is known to be a vital tool in helping people control the brain as well as the thoughts of others. To solidify a concept in someone's mind, you need to repeat it as many times as possible. Use the repetition approach for your advantage, and you will have access to someone's brain without them having a clue of it. Do not feel afraid of repeating your idea again and again. Thinking that you might offend them by your repetition will be the worst thing to do. Put your plan in different versions and making them clear but make sure it is a similar thing. The repeating will combine with the feeling of the brain relaxation, and give your idea the chance to become real. Make your interlocutor believe that the reality you are fighting for is a better option and the best they could hop.

Practice Being Positive

Everybody loves feeling good, and nobody likes to be associated with conflicts as well as difficulties. To make your interlocutor not resist your suggestion, whatever you suggest need to look positive. Your positivity will make them put their guard down, and you will control their mind without their knowledge. Make your ideas look as high as possible and demonstrate how they will end up into achieving success. The positive technique makes you look supportive, even when you may not be. Engage in positive interacting, and no should not be an answer. A negative reply can act as a powerful distraction, and it will not give you the ability to control the other person's thought. Give yes for an answer even if you know that the results will be negative. That will make the people around you think that you re supportive as well as thoughtful. Spinning things toward the possible will lead you in achieving your desired results without the other person knowing that you are controlling their mind.

Maintain a Harmonious Relationship

After you can capture, the attention of your subject, increase the rapport? Give your hidden suggestions as well as embodied commands and make sure they embrace them. Tell them what you require of them without directly addressing the need. Going direct to the exact thing that you want them to do will trigger their curiosity and make them think critically. If they get active in thinking, your entire plan to control their mind may go into ruin. You will have lost your control on them which is not your primary aim. Use the best suitable methods to strengthen the link and make sure that your interlocutor to trust you. When they believe you, they will have no difficulty in putting their confidence in you.

Seek to Know What Motivates Them

You need to find out what is making some people choose their opinions instead of yours. When you understand them from this point of view, you will have the know-how on the best way to handle them. When you know the exact thing that motivates them, you will find that ground for your advantage. Controlling them after knowing what makes them happy will make you go great miles. Once you understand what motivates them, you will influence the motivations by persuading them to try something different. The different thing they need to work should be your own opinion. The simplest way to find out what motivates them is seeking an explanation of why they prefer a specific idea over the other. Pay full attention to what they have to say, and it will be appropriate if you watch their non-verbal response. You not only need to focus on what motivates them but look into the most powerful motivator. Their most crucial motivator will give a clue on how you need to put your point across. Manipulating this motivator will be the easiest as well as the best strategy to help you in controlling their minds. What they give the most value when it comes to decision making will be of great importance. Try and remember the steps that they have used before to make decisions and try to manipulate them. If you know what their motivator is, you can present to them in the best way possible. It has an assurance that you will take control over their minds as well as thoughts, and they will not know of it.

Create Confidence

You must let your interlocutor view themselves as being the hero. It serves as an excellent way to convince them to do what you want without them noticing you have taken control. Demonstrate to your interlocutor their perception matters in your context. When you achieve having their confidence, you will address anything to them with a lot of ease. Tell them how important it would be for them to be directly involved in your ideas. You need to tell them that they will own the credit once the ideas become successful. You will have taken control of the person mind since all humans are pleased with any situation that will make them bring glory. Let the interlocutor feel that they play a vital role, and things cannot progress without their involvement. Show them that their presence is all that is required to get things moving. People need to feel a sense of belonging, and they will let down their guards quickly. After feeling they belong, they will be willing to open up and be free to you. Opening up will give you direct control to their mind, and they will not realize even an inch. Help them see that the contribution they are about to make will not go unnoticed. Make sure they don't understand that you have an ulterior motive; instead; you want to lend a helping hand because you value them. It needs to be real as possible, and it would be necessary to avoid any exploitative circumstance for your security. Make your way to look the safest and that you will be responsible for any shortcoming. They will have confidence in you when they know that you are sure of what you are talking. Being kind to a person will make them feel safe to open up to you and let their mind known to you. The more they open up, the more you find a way to manipulate as well as control them. They may not have an idea that you are controlling them since they find it right to open up. Be firm as well as confident and do not belittle their views no matter how tiny they seem to be.

Make Use of Their Emotions

There is an approach that you can apply how somebody feels so that you can control them. When someone has mixed feelings, they may not know that they are monitoring them. They will do what you want being propelled by what they feel. You can use a situation that you know has addicted your interlocutor to make them do what you desire. Anger can as well be an excellent weapon to take control over someone. Use a wise way that will not alarm them of your aim to induce irritation in your interlocutor. When the person has anger boiling, they can comply with whatever they are told to do. They can do that out of revenge or finding a way to cool them down. They will blame their anger, and they will not know that you are using them for your gain. Involving ego and making the person see that they may lose their ego if they do not do a particular thing will make them comply. When you assure them that their ego too will increase, they will submit with no second thought. Telling someone that the community is expecting them to fail will make them put more efforts so that they prove that community wrong. The idea of getting their ego involved will work best when you are dealing with an arrogant person. The ones who have an inflated ego will as well be controlled easily without noticing. Creating as well as inducing fear in someone will be an excellent plan to manage them. Fear will give you access to the interlocutor's thoughts as well as the mind, and they will act out of fear. You will get to your intended aim when you use fear as a technique. Another way of controlling a person using their emotions is by making them feel guilty. When someone feels guilty, they will find all means possible to make it up to you. In the process, you can control their mind since they have no say when it comes to paying you back.

Inducing an emotion to someone will make them act in a particular way. You need to understand the person, and you will be in a position to lead them to any direction you feel. When your interlocutor is emotional, you will not put in more efforts to control their mind since that will come automatically. Emotions can make a personal sacrifice a lot for the person they value. You can as well use your feelings to play along with someone's brain for your advantage. All you need to do is pretend that a particular thing has affected you emotionally and the next party will automatically be sympathetic, at such a situation, you can present your ideas, and they will have no objection considering your position at the moment. Guilt is known to be more effective than making someone angry. Anger may have a negative effect, while guilt may favor you.

So that you can gain control of someone's mind, you need to have an understanding of their personality. The knowledge of your interlocutor character will help you know the approach to use to gain control over their mind. You will know how they will react when in a particular emotional situation. Some people tend to be more explosive than others, and you need to know how to handle them when conditions get tough. Some are easy to control while others require you to put in more effort to bring them under your control. The need to manage a person may not always be as a way of being mean. Some of the reasons may be healthy and of help to both parties. You need to be cautious when trying to control a person's mind. When they realize that you want to control them, they can object or turn to be hostile towards you. That means that the relationship between both of you will be affected. They might as well try to avoid you after that thinking that you are a threat to their life.

Chapter 6: Techniques to Influence People

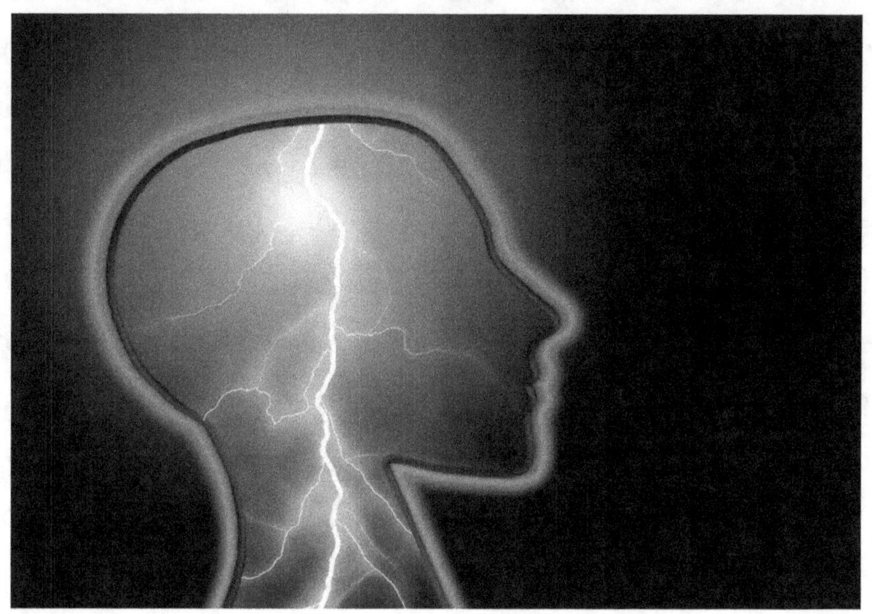

The way you associate with people not only determine the relationship you are likely to have, but also the influence you have on them. How you influence people will learn how they respond to you. Dealing with people in the right way will give you a ground to alter them in any way you desire. You will tend to blame others unnecessarily if you do not know how to deal with them. You may think that people are mean to you while you cannot handle as well as influence them. Any response that people will give to you tend to be your responsibility. Different approaches will derive different results. The method that you will decide to use to influence other people will determine the kind of response you will get. The terms you use will affect how others will react. If you want to change people, you need to assume the responsibility for the results. If you receive undesirable effects that mean that you used the wrong technique to influence people. Some people will use the wrong way to control people despite them knowing the best way to use. When you don't view reality in the right direction, you cannot manage to influence people. Do not assume that people are arrogant by their outward appearance. The wrong impression will give you an unpleasant response from the person. Do not judge people based on false beliefs you may be having on them. Nevertheless, there are several ways that you can use to influence even the most charismatic person. They include;

Maintain Confidence

Confidence is vital when it comes to any situation. Being confident will guarantee the other person that you are sure of whatever you have to say or do. When you lose your confidence, automatically, the next party cannot trust you as well. To influence any person, you need to portray the character of an active person. Confidence will gain you more marks, and any person will give you a chance to present your ideas which they are likely to embrace. Maintain an eye to eye contact while talking with a person is a sign of confidence and an assurance you know what you are doing. Your non-verbal forms of communication play an essential role in showing whether you are optimistic. The standing posture you use will either confirm your confidence or lack of faith. The movements that you make and your positioning around someone will talk much about you. It might betray you or not, and it will determine whether you will influence a person or not. You need to control your emotions not to express them unknowingly. For that, you need to maintain calmness at its best. You can opt to use mindfulness to monitor the body language to avoid the person to doubt you. Speak softly to capture their attention and maintain calmness in the movements you are likely to make. Controlling the speed that you talk with will make you sound calmer as well as brighter. If you cannot speak at a slow pace, you need to consider learning how to by practicing quiet talk. You can do this by reading aloud at a plodding pace. Keep away from any signs of a confronting body language like maintaining eye contact for more extended periods. Have neutral face expressions; avoid aggressive gestures, or even standing directly opposite the person.

Change your Strategy

It is necessary to know the strategy to use to approach someone so that your aim to influence them can succeed. You need to have a room of change when there is a need. You will use different strategies to deal with different people and the need to be flexible. In the end, you will get to know the plan that works and the one that does not. Your ultimate goal should be to influence the other person positively. It is well to consider the results of the thing you are about to do in case your plan does not go in the way you expected.

Try and predict what the other person is likely to say next.

Offer them their Choice

If you aim at influencing people, offering them what they want and not what you want will work perfectly well. You need to forget about yourself and focus on what makes them happy. When you focus on the other person and what their interests are, you will change their view about you, and they will start viewing you as the right person. That is what you require to influence people. They will respect you more and as well give you the power when you provide them with actually what they want. People tend to care about their interest and using the technique of giving them what their interest is will work excellently. To influence people, give them what they desire to have. For you to change people of any caliber, offer them what they want and they will obey you without you having to use much power.

Make the Person feel Important

If you make someone feel that they matter and they are of importance, they will do anything for you. It plays a vital role in influencing people and making them do what you want. You cannot force someone to do what you want unless you lure them to doing it. And making them feel you appreciate them is the best way to bring them under your control. Tell them that they are of importance in your life. Demonstrate how life will be incomplete without them playing a part. They need to know that you acknowledge their help always. That will make them obey and do things with passion and embrace you for who you are.

Work for an Emotional Connection

When you compact emotionally to someone, they will go things for you without you necessarily asking them to do. They will be self-driven and will work to please you all the times. When you have an emotional connection, you will be more understanding. Getting to understand what the next person feels gives them the confidence that you care. They tend to lower their guard, and you gain access to influencing them. If you connect someone's emotions to specific goals, it will help them move to the next level. Helping them go from one level to the other will make them trust you and view you as a leader, and that will make you win them. Connecting will make people go to the extra mile to make sure that they achieve the best with you. For this, you need to be connected emotionally with the same agenda for you to achieve success.

Empower them

You are likely to gain authority when you empower people. Gaining power over them means that you will influence them in any direction that you desire. Finding ways to motivate them will give them the feeling that you care for their welfare. What you make people feel will forever remain in their mind and will leave a permanent mark. Making them think that they are the only ones that matter will make you have a significant influence on what they do. Start empowering people, and you will be in a position to influence them. For people to embrace change, you need to enable them, and you will gain power over them. Empowering your mates is as well a sign that you are a successful person.

Respect the other Person's Opinion

Never view the other person's opinion as wrong. And the worst mistake that you can do is admitting to them that they are wrong. It is wise for you to respect their opinion, no matter whether it is right or wrong. Everyone thinks that they are right in everything they do and pinning them down by showing how wrong they are will make them change the view of who you are. When they give a contribution that is not correct, confirm them that you respect their opinion despite you having a different perspective. Tell them how you think in respect to the entire thing and do it in a wise way not to offend them. When you respect people's opinion, they will be free with you to the extent of letting you influence them. No matter what the character of a person can be, they always respect anyone who pays attention to their opinion. And not only respecting but respecting without criticizing openly. Nobody likes to criticism regardless of what they have done. Embracing their view is an essential approach for you to use to be in a position to influence them.

Be a Leader

To influence people, you need to be a leader and not a boss. The character traits of a leader will make you work together on projects, visions as well as goals as a team, instead of ordering people around. Getting involved in implementing ideas and not ordering people to do that as you watch will create a good rapport between you and the people around you. A good rapport will then result in a good relationship, and in that way, you will influence people without having to sweat for it. Empower people as you coordinate them if you want to control them. Ordering people around will ruin your chances to influence them since no one likes a person with the character of a boss. A leader will pay attention to what the juniors are saying and will not dismiss them anyhow. They will seek ideas on how to do a particular thing and will involve everyone in decision making. That will make people feel included and, that is all that is needed to make things flow smoothly. There is no given time that they will think they are more superior to the rest. They will always seek the opinion of the others and will not make anyone feel out of place. When you practice being a boss, people will talk ill about you, but when you be a leader, they will always praise you. People avoid getting into a conflict with a leader because of the respect they have for him or her. To have significant influence, make sure there is smooth as well as efficient communication between you and the people around you.

Be Sympathetic

Have sympathy and never scold someone if they make a mistake but always remember that they can make a mistake since they are human beings. Let your main aim be to help people not to repeat an error instead of punishing them. Your prime purpose should be to help others and hurt them. Do not sting people, and you need to find a friendly approach to use when dealing with a mistake so that you can influence them. You have to help them understand that they are on the wrong track without hurting their feelings. Show them that you have also made mistakes in the past and you are not perfect. But you had to change for the best, and this will show a sign of sympathy. Demonstrate to them the need not to repeat that for the second time and give them a vote of confidence that they will not do that the next time.

Be Assertive

Being aggressive will harm than good. Being confident is among the best ways to influence people, no matter their character. Aggressiveness shows arrogance which most people do not appreciate at any given time. Present your ideas as well as thoughts with confidence and indicate your convictions. It is crucial to make sure that you are not overconfident because that shows that someone is arrogant in one way or the other. That will compromise your ability to influence people instead.

You need to take caution, especially when you do not know the audience you have to engage. Embrace assertiveness as quality to help you interact with people as well as build a reputation. It needs to be this way regardless of the person you are dealing with. The primary purpose is to influence them, and that should be what you are focusing on all the time. Believe in the things that you say, and that will help you cultivate authority over people. You will earn influence on them with o hard pushing.

Lend a Listening Ear

Influencing is two-way and involving the people around you will work correctly. Make sure you incorporate their opinions in your vision as a way to show that you believe in them. They too, will find in your views and combine them with theirs to make the thing run smoothly. For you to enhance such a relationship with people, you have to listen to them. Encouraging them to talk about their minds and to give their ideas always. They should not fear to express what they think will be of benefit to the people. When people don't get a chance to make contributions, it would be wise for you to turn the tables and give them that chance to express their views. Respect as well as acknowledge their opinions and let them know you value them, and they matter to you. An atmosphere of trust, respect as well as mutual teamwork will take control, giving you the advantage to influence people. Spearhead the initiative to create such an environment, and they will view you as a leader and a boss. As discussed earlier, leaders always have their way to influence people while bosses do not manage. When you present an idea, they will embrace it as well as acknowledge and respect the result.

Do not be Defensive

You need to be calm in a possible way since arrogance will do more harm than good. To be able to influence a person, you need to be convincing in the right direction. Do not claim the ownership of every small that goes on. Taking credit where you do not deserve will only make things worse.

Avoid Arguments

Disagree with people will trigger you emotionally, and you might end up messing up. If you are not able to win their trust, there is no way you are going to influence them. Avoid any situation that may lead to compromises and making you angry along. Arguing will make it harder for you to win the heart of any person.

Influence is known as a unique asset in the executive world, but you need to keep in mind that you aim to influence people and nothing else. Do not use this as a way to gain fame or for your advantage. Let it be a chance to the benefit of everyone around you. Achieving influence is critical to attaining success since control is a strength. You will work as well as relate more effectively if you gain control on people. Power produces respect as well as appreciation and will give your opinions a voice. The best thing is to use the approaches to gain influence positively, and you will hit your aim. You can influence even the most charismatic people if you play your cards in a recommendable way.

Chapter 7: All We Have Is a Dark Side

92

Have you ever thought yourself of creating a negative impact of this life? Sometimes people are engrossed with the right things or morals they have and forget their dark sides. Other scenarios are where one is prized highly even by parents that you value yourself of a higher standard than your counterparts. That feeling is sometimes unfortunate because you may think you are right in anything whereas other individuals see our weakness. That is why it is good to accept all corrections as one cannot identify their ills or wrongs unless you are told.

What about the dark side you have? You may be surprised to know that the dark side in you can be used as an advantage. Sometimes one is too proud to recognize the vices one have. Other people know their vices, and they feel pressured to control them, therefore generating a personality disorder. You may be that guy who is always viewed to be wicked; thus, everybody fears from that character in you. You, therefore, feel isolated and think you cannot do anything to change their perception on you.

Another instance is that you may have been involved in a sorrowful ordeal. Your past tends to determine the life course one chooses. You feel that you cannot try a particular task because you failed once, and you believe you are a complete failure. Maybe at one time, you were short-tempered at an extent of injuring your friend or sibling with a machete. Therefore, you will grow with the attitude that there is a hidden darkness in you.

In some cases, this is the demonic part in you, and you should try to control it in every way. Many relationships have broken because the partners did not take time to know the evil of the other. All they shared is their bright linen, and they did not take time to understand the dirty linen of the other spouse. It would be hurting to know the prince charming or the queen you once believed can hart you in a way you never expected.

Therefore, it is suitable for everybody to recognize the demonic part of you and try to share with anyone who can understand. Moreover, before getting in a relationship, dig at the background to identify the weakness of your beloved. Everybody has the evil spirit inside which you may know or do not. Do you ever think your enemies can ever tell you something positive? But consider asking them of what they hate you for, you may realize they do not hate you but dislikes the vice in you. You may further be surprised that they want you to change for the better. It is essential to know who your real friends are because some are fake friends. They will relate with you to discover your weakness of which they will exploit you negatively.

Having that evil side is sometimes a positive thing because you will know your true nature. Sometimes you are afraid that your close friend will discover your dark side and laugh at you. At other times you like living alone because you feel the demon in you will harm the people you care. Such people experience low self-esteem and do not see any value in themselves. However, there is good news. do you know even the best of you may be the dark side to other people? You may be that bright guy in school or that star player but do you know too much of anything is poisonous. You are used to being praised or celebrated by your colleagues, therefore you developed that arrogance attitude. Hence that is an evil nature in you.

How Can One Use the Evil Nature in You for Your Advantage?

You use that character one has to know who your real friends are. The worst betrayal is that which comes from close friends. That pal of yours may not even love you but as waiting at that moment you. Sometimes these friends are interested in the possessions or the richness you have, but when poverty strikes you, they will eclipse. Kings or queens are followed because of the influence, wealth, and authority they commission to that kingdom, but not out of the love the subjects have for them. Your dark nature in you will disconnect you from fake friends and connect you to real allies.

This feeling helps one to have an attitude of self-acceptance. Maybe you have done everything to stop these evils. However, your hustles are fruitless. You eventually feel that it is an epidemic that you cannot fight. However, by realizing your true nature, you will consequently learn that attitude to accept yourself. Therefore, you can face people in confidentially as you feel you have the power to control that evilness you have.

Being weak and feeling disoriented in society is another negative impact of the dark side in you. However, if you learn to manage those feelings, you will have no more fear to face society. You will undoubtedly identify those people who are ready to support you and finish that distrust you possess. Sometimes you may have done wrong that you fear of repeating such actions. Consequently, you even fear yourself, but if you do self-evaluation, you will stop that attitude.

Sometimes the evilness in you can help you to attain you want. You can be dictatorial in any way, but that attitude will command respect and obedient from your subordinates. They will fear you and will try to do everything right to please you. You always have a negative attitude in everything, but you will be a winner if your optimistic friend loses in an area he thought was achievable. If people fear that you will hurt them, they will allow you to do everything that pleases you.

Some scholars say that you can only 'solve evil with evil.' This ideology works when one wants to reduce the vices found in society. You are that saint whom everybody respects, but how can you fight those criminals who fight you if you do not know how they think. Therefore, if you have a Dark side, you will learn about it and recognize how to deal with it. Therefore, if your counterpart has the same element you will be in a position to manage him. That is why most people use reformed addicts or criminals to advise other individuals suffering under the same umbrella.

How Can One Use the Dark Side To Manipulate People?

Many are the cases people are conned, and they often say that the culprit manipulated them. This move can go to an extent where a person is coerced or brainwashed to do something of, not their wish. Manipulation in some people can be viewed as a vice that is not acceptable. It is usually a way of influencing, coercing or persuading a person to agree with what you want. In this case, you are the dominant force, and your counterpart is the less dominant person. Many of the manipulators use different approaches in eliciting you to do what they want. Some may be sweet-talking to influence you to do something that even you did not wish to. Others will forcefully blackmail you or corer you to do a favor,

Manipulation is an example of the dark side that you may possess. Being manipulated sometimes show that you are gullible, and you can easily be fooled to do something that you never wished. Those particular people who influence others are mostly the emotional intelligent guys. Such personnel plays around with your feelings and you sense danger you do not follow their instructions. One may ask how the dark nature in you is connected to manipulation. Remember that manipulation may be positive or negative, but in this case, consider manipulation in positive grounds. If you are a parent, you must show you wrong side so that the children can obey you. Imagine how you feared to do wrong when you were a kid because you were afraid of caning from parents. Therefore, the parents will manipulate you in doing something right by using such painful measures. Isn't that the right side of manipulation prompted by the dark side?

What are Yin and Yang

It is a Chinese philosophy that shows how contrary parties or opposite ones may intermingle, connect, and interdepend on each other. You will always feel oriented to mingle with another even if you do not share the same class. This principality is associated with the dark nature one has. Yin is expressed and marked as evil, wicked, feminist, and shadows. While Yang is marked as bright, masculinity, heaven, and eminence, these two groups of people usually relate to energize their colleague. Recognize that Yang is mostly associated with male and Yin is associated with females.

It has been found that both of these qualities very differently and are used in manipulation. A Yin person is characterized by being a listener, softy, coolness, surrender, and respectful. In Yang people, they are portrayed in being brave, authoritative, and strict. Therefore, in most cases, the Yang People Influences the Yin individuals

Ten Ways Manipulators Use Their Dark Sides

Manipulators mostly cheat to gain an advantage over you. The specific issues that they mainly cheat are to generate pity from you. They will lie about a particular episode that happened to them, and they will try to connect that story on what they aim you to perform. Therefore, you will feel motivated by what they want to do to prevent such a terrible episode from happening to you. Think of a person who tells you not to walk on a particular street because burglars attacked him. You will surely not walk on that path. Therefore, without knowing the person will influence you to walk on the road he or she wants.

They mostly instill your fear. These individuals like warning their victims which is a way of instilling phobia on doing something you are meant to do. For the case of that street, they scare you like 'burglars will attack you if you follow the same path I followed.' It is the nature of a being to fear the danger or horrifying scenes. Therefore, they use such weakness of people to their advantage. They may even fake a story or use an illustration of the sad story of a person who followed the path they do not want you to take. You will undoubtedly try to avoid such episodes, and hence you will fall in their trap.

These people can identify when you're happy and take advantage of that situation. Happiness is a good thing for every human, which one aims to have. Every activity that one does or practices the most significant priority is to achieve maximum happiness. They can do soothing that will make you jovial as a way of capturing your attention. Whenever you are in discussion with them, they will jump to that topic which they perceive is interesting to you. You will undoubtedly hear them out after you realize they focus on things that entice you. Without knowing they will use that chance to influence to fulfill their wishes. Imagine hearing a person singing the song you like you will undoubtedly stop what you are doing to hear them out.

Manipulators always like blackmailing their victims. That is where they use the reciprocity rule when engaging you. This rule states that do unto others as they have done for you. If maybe you are in job interviewing panel and you realize someone buys you some presents before the interview. Know that the particular person wants to manipulate you to favor him in job recruitment. What if you take their valuable gifts which you cannot afford to compensate them, you will only be left with one choice, which is that you will have to favor them. Therefore, if you realize such people, please do not accept their presents or gifts.

These folks always want to be the center of the conversation. They like painting a picture that they know much than you. Even when you are conversing with them, they will try to put much vocabulary and jargon to make you look inferior. By doing this, you will develop the fear of criticizing them and correcting them. They always seek for influence and dominates amid the conversation you have. You can even create an attitude that they know better than you, hence everything they say you will find it right and intelligent. The route they want you to follow, you will undoubtedly observe that path. To manage such people, it is essential to have a neutral talk where all of you have the same say. Whenever you feel that they are trying to gain dominance, cut the story off, and remind them that you share the same grounds.

These persons always ask lots of questions. They ask such questions when they give you less space to answer. You will realize that they still talk to fast that you cannot easily comprehend what they are saying. Hey, that is a scheme they develop to hide their real intention. The questions will be based on your failures, where they want to discover such weaknesses to blackmail you. They want to talk fast so that they can blame you that you are the one not listening well. Allowing you to criticize them or correct them will expose evil schemes which is something they would not love.

These people always want you to look like the villain in any terrible story. They want you to feel like you are the guilty one in any situation. They will cite an episode you were involved in and try to show you that you are the one who made a mistake. They use such a weapon because they know that it is human nature to try to justify themselves. Therefore, they give you a platform to excuse yourself from an ordeal where they place their demands as a mean of that justification. Therefore, you will surely do what they want to remove your dirty linen out of the public sight.

Showing their negative emotions is one way to trick you into doing what they require. They may even fake a sentiment that will touch you. They can feign anger, sorrowfulness, remorse, and other emotions. Remember they want to gain control of your feelings. Imagine how what would you do if your beloved kid threatens to kill himself if you do not buy him the promise. You will surely be manipulated to buy him that toy, where the kid was faking that emotion as it is impossible for the child to kill himself.

Sometimes these individuals want to show you that they are favoring you more than others. Whenever they award you with something, they will whisper how they preferred you in that situation. They will tell you that you have impressed them in a certain way and they feel obliged to return the favor. They want you to look superior over others as is the nature of a person to feel praised above others. Therefore, you will be enticed to do what they want so that they can keep on complementing you often.

Chapter 8: Advanced Techniques for Mind Hacking

In the recent past, hackers have assumed a lousy reputation in the tech-heavy world. In other words, their activities entail the art of logging into systems without permission and offering illegal commands. The aspect has been detrimental in the sense that organizations have been losing funds, let alone the confidence they have over their customers. However, according to Sir John Hargrave, human beings are all hackers, that is mind hackers. The art is linked to the fact that as human beings can effectively recognize certain situations and control the focus of one`s minds concerning the subject in question. In mind hacking, it is not just about thinking. It involves the art of thinking and rethinking about what one of streamlining off. Thus, Hargrave claims that one can rethink and write the code behinds the thoughts therein. In other words, mind hacking entails the detailed re-cap of what the mind has been thinking. For the accounts to be active, one has to apply some crucial techniques effectively.

Take a look at some of the techniques you can use to enhance practical mind thinking.

Upgrade yourself.

In most cases, when one gets to a training session, one mind may get to wonder and fail to focus on a specific target. However, one needs to refocus and return their attention to the primary goal. It is worth noting that the art of being attentive might be challenging to maintain following many common distractions. It is critical to note that with practice, one can sustain attention and ignore a lot of entertainment that might progressively stay for more extended periods and causing the loss of focus. As a mind hacker, one may log out to what is said to be user mode. It is also possible to log back into what is termed as super-user mode where one can rewire the brains and become more productive and effective.

According to Harvey, the art of logging out of the system is not a problem. However, the major problem is where one logs out of the system without their knowledge. In such situations, training becomes effective where one train on how to remain in the super-user mode for more extended periods and become more productive. In other words, through the art of training, one can keep the mind in the super-user mode, learn more about what they are thinking and become more effective in whatever they are doing.

Think of attention like Money

The art of focusing your attention to the mind is like putting one`s money in a bank account with some compound interest. It is worth noting that it requires Money for one to make more money. In the same way, if you want to be attentive, you need to use your attention and remain focused. Scholars have identified that focus is one of the most scarce aspects or commodity in life. Thus, one ought to be careful and work on maintaining this powerful resource that life has offered.

Avoid Attention Fragmentation

There have been studies that have been carried to investigate how active people are as they multitask. However, the results have adequately indicated that the art of multitasking weakens the minds ability to concentrate and remain focused. In other words, people who multitask filter out irrelevancy in most cases. In other words, since their minds aren't focused on what they are doing, their products tend to below, and the results are always sick. The art of multitasking or rather attention fragmentation causes one to explore a lot of things and yet become a master of none. In other words, the one weakens the mind and the ability to focus on the most productive aspects of life is lost; hence, the achievement of poor results. It is worth noting that Excellency requires one to be focused on a particular aspect of life and avoid being swayed by issues. The other demerit about fragmentation is that it steals one ability to recall items. In other words, one unable to manage memories and my end up forgetting the essential things in life. One is easily distracted and may not be able to recover what they have been doing once they lose their concentration.

In most cases, once they are distracted, they are unable to recover their initial position, and they are forced to restarts gain. For instance, is one was working in a particular experiment, and multitasking, there are chances that if they are distracted, they will probably forget the step they were in and end up restarting again once they recover. The aspect is devastating in the sense that it wastes time and resources as well. However, you need to be focused and stick to one task. The element is critical in the sense that it allows one to channel all their energies to a particular aspect of life and get better results rather than multitasking with the aim of achieving a lot within a short period and end up losing everything when things are messed up. Thus, make a point of deliberating on your attention and remain being focused.

Booking Habits with Rewards and Cues

These are essential habits that are critical in life. Such practices are vital in the sense that they allow one to be more productive and effective in life. For instance, the art of being consistent is very critical in life. If you want to cement a particular habit in your life, you need to be consistent and it times of time and place. Choose a suitable moment, for instance, in the morning when you aren't tired. There are cases where you might have to select a location that will suit you best. For example. You can choose a reminder such as a digital clock that will keep reminding of the habit you want to cement. The approach is critical in the sense that it allows one to remain focused and productive. The other aspect that is crucial in cementing a habit is the use of rewards. You need to reward yourself once you have been able to cement the practice for some time. It is worth noting that most of these aspects are more of a mind-set. Thus, you can effectively hack your mind and cement a particular habit in life that is worth noting.

Tracking your Mind

In most cases, it takes time for the minds to be tuned to a particular aspect of life and remain cemented for a more extended period. In other words, it requires patience and consistency for cementation of a habit. Essential habits require more energy than bad habits. However, the art of starting a bad habit is very firsts; however, leaning them is very challenging. The art developing a specific concept requires one to be consistent in the way they do things.

In most cases, if the habit isn't well acknowledged or embraced, one may easily forget about it. Thus, the best thing that one can do is to establish a chart that will help one follow on the progress. The aspect is critical in the sense that it keeps one focused and attentive on achieving better results.

Writing

Until something is in papers, it is vapor. In other words, once you have practiced new ideas, you need to put them down in an article. The aspect is critical in the sense that it allows one to be sober and keep remembering about the new concepts made. It is worth noting that writing is the gateway behind one`s mind.

In other words, the thoughts in most cases become the things as well as the ideas that are brought from the head to the hands. For instance, if you want to lose weight, the best thing is to adopt a particular concept of life and work on via writing. If you decide to utilize the diet as a significant way of reducing your weight, come up with a time table that will help you open up. Planning is best done via writing. The aspect allows participants to maintain a record of all that is happening. For instance, one may record the way they have been reducing weight over time. The aspect allows one to keep working. In other words, a record of the progress is critical in the sense that it will enable one to check in the improvement achieved as well as the issues that need to be addressed. It is essential to understand that one can appreciate a specific habit of seeing the results. For instance, one may realize having adopted jogging following after seeing that they have improved in terms of their weight as well as their health. The habit will thus be cemented in their minds, and they won`t deviate from it quickly.

Operate it as an Addiction

The art of addiction is considered to be a life-long disease that affects the way a person behaves or think.

Thus, professionals promote the utilization of drugs that are causing the brain to re-organize itself and form new neural connections. In most cases, people who are addicted to specific issues of life have their minds tuned to their habits more permanently. For instance, alcohol addicts, at times, fail to be active before they are drunk. However, if the addict rewires their brain and makes deliberate decisions to avoiding their habits, they become more productive and maintain soberness. Thus, most of the things or rather the practices we engage in are wired in the brain. If one wants to achieve a particular aspect of life, repetition is vital. In other words, you may have to plan your time well and enhance repetition within your activities. You may have to plan your entire day and ensure that you establish a habit that will help you achieve what you want. In other words, you need to avoid a negative lope in your life by outlining some of the practices or activities you want to be achieved within a specified period. You need to avoid all the negative minds in your life and work on the things that make you feel good. Record all the achievements and learn to appreciate the simple steps of life you are making.

Sit with Optimistic People

It is worth noting that if you sit around negative people, there are chances that you will give up and start working on other things. However, if you sit around optimistic people, they will encourage what you are doing and help you work out well. Positive people will always try and help you understand the importance of doing certain things in a certain way. For instance, they will help you avoid addiction or rather stay positive. They will help you become the best of you rather than discourage you. Such people are critical in the sense that they will help you set your objectives and help you achieve them. Some will repeatedly encourage you and help you formulate some vital schemes. Most of them have more significant experience, and they know what it takes to be positive and the results of having the right approach. They are the kind of individuals who will outline some of the benefits of achieving a particular aspect of life.

In most cases, they will help you commit your time and resources so as you may achieve a particular aspect. Thus, as you plan to change your mind-set, make a point of associating yourself with people who are relevant in your life. There is no need of having people who are negative in your life, yet you need to achieve the best. There is no need for seeking guidance or rather opinion from people who have been failures. In other words, you need to seek advice from people who are doing great in life and work as per their guidelines. In other words, there is no way you can stop a specific addiction by sitting around with people who are addicted to the same habit. They will easily distract you and corrupt your minds as well. However, if you sit across people who were once addicted and have effectively avoided the addiction, you will be able to achieve more and avoid it easily.

A Constant Reminder

A reminder is anything that will help remember a particular aspect at a specific period. For instance, if you are planning to avoid an absolute addiction, you may have to replace the activity with something else. The aspect will thus force you to have a constant reminder that will always remind you of the things that need to be done. The reminder will help you move from the addict and work on avoiding it. Also, if you are planning on running each morning, there are chances that you may not fully embrace the issue at the beginning. During such moments, a constant reminder is required. You may also need to write something either on your computer or on the wall of the house such that you will always remember that there is something you need to achieve. You need to create reminders that will stick in your minds. For instance, if you want to stop smoking, you can write something like smoking is illegal in this house. The aspect allows one to be active and plan well. Such a reminder will easily stick in one`s brain. You may also have to put the reminder in a familiar place such as the washroom, or around your dining area. The aspect is critical in the sense that it allows one to keep posted of the habit or addiction that needs to be avoided. You may also have to formulate formulas or acronyms that will help you remember what you need to do. Also, plan to succeed and fix it in your minds.

Starting Small

There is no way you can achieve something once. For instance, if you are want to lower your body weight through running, there are no ways you can run for the first time and expect a change. However, some of these habits require one to be patient and employ the art of being positive and consistent. In most cases, starting small allows one to learn. If you notice you are getting right, make a point of getting the right things being done as fast as possible. However, for the things that are not immediate, you may have to train your minds and work progressively. In other words, the achievement of certain aspects of life requires the utilization of brains as well as other body systems such as immunity. It is worth noting that such systems can't` be adjusted promptly. However, one requires to be patient and consistent. The aspect is critical in the sense that it opens one to new ideas and achieve them with ease. Such behaviors capture the minds if an individual and there are no ways one may think of otherwise. When the thoughts are effectively captured, they will be easily be manipulated in what Harvey calls mind-hacking. Thus, one can achieve anything in this life so long as their minds are wired to positivity and will power.

Chapter9: Develop Your Dark Personality and Become a Puppet Master of the Minds of Others

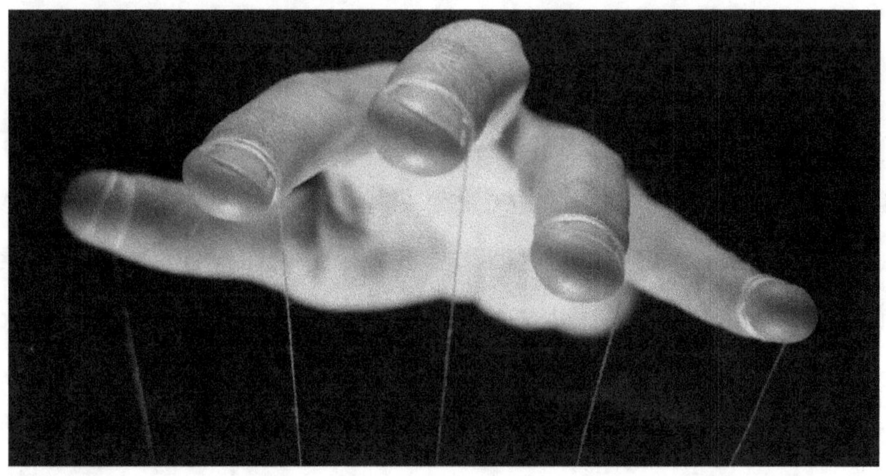

Using dark personality to control and manipulate others is something that happens in our lives every day. Psychologists refer to it as psychological manipulation which is a form of social influence with the objective of changing other people's perception and even behavior. This can be achieved by using deception, indirectness, and other underhand tactics. The manipulator, in this case, advances their own interests at other people's expense through using exploitative and devious means.

It is important to take note that social influence is not necessarily bad or negative. There are other aspects of social influence that are positive and encouraged by cultures across the world. A good example is where friends, family or colleagues persuade their member to change from bad behavior which may negatively impact on them. When social influence respects the right of the influenced person and no deception or coercion is used on them, then such influence is generally perceived to be harmless.

Dark Psychology and manipulation

Psychology tends to study human behavior by focusing on important factors such as our actions, thoughts, and social interactions. Dark psychology, on the other hand, focuses on mind control and manipulation. The term Dark Triad is often used by psychologists and criminologists to study and understand important issues such as broken relationships, and criminal behavior in society.

Narcissistic people in society use their dark personality traits such as lack of empathy, egotism, and grandiosity to take advantage of other people. Machiavellianism uses pure manipulation to exploit as well as deceive other people. These people also have no sense of morality at all. Psychopaths on their part use charm and being friendly but inwardly are selfish, full of impulsivity and lack any form of remorse.

No one wants to fall prey to being manipulated, however, sometimes we find ourselves being in such situations without really knowing it. We may not be a victim of someone specific in the dark triad, however, you may fall victim to dark psychology tactics almost daily.

Everyday Scenarios of Manipulation

Love Flooding

One of the common tactics of manipulation we come across on a daily basis is 'love flooding'. Love flooding refers to complimenting someone, showing affection and buttering someone in order to place a request. For example, we may show love and affection to a loved one or become 'overly' affectionate with them in order to ask for a favor. This kind of 'manipulation' is quite common in families and marriages.

Lying

Another common form of manipulation in all cultures and societies is lying. You have certainly been lied to by someone who wanted to get a favor from you. Conversely, you may have at one point lied to someone to get something out of them. A good example is where children lie to their parents about completing their assignments when asked about it when in the real sense they have not done it. Lying may consist of untrue stories, exaggerations, partial truths, half-truths or withholding the whole truth.

Love denial

Love denial consists of withholding affection and attention. This is another example of everyday manipulation that many people go through. A person may withhold affection to another person as a way of manipulating them to act or behave in a certain way. This is a form of manipulation because withholding affection is often a powerful motivator that jolts someone to act in a certain way, often the manipulator's way.

Reverse Psychology

This is a very common method of manipulation in which the manipulator asks someone through persuasion to do something by asking them to do the opposite. According to psychologists, reverse psychology relies on a phenomenon called 'reactance theory'. Reactance theory involves taking away 'power and control' from someone. People don't like this and when put in such situations, they will do anything to get this control back even if what they are about to do goes against their interests. This is what manipulators bank on when employing reverse control.

Semantic manipulation

You can also use semantic manipulation to manipulate someone into acting or behaving in a particular way. Semantic manipulation involves using words that seem to have a mutual definition. In this case, the manipulator says something and the victim thinks that they have the same meaning, only later does the manipulator reveal to them that he had a different definition and understanding of the conversation they had.

Which people use manipulation tactics?

Everyone has one time or the other used manipulation to get something. However, there are certain people in societies who are prone to using manipulation more than 'normal' people do. Below are some examples of people in society who by nature or by the virtue of their jobs use forms of manipulation frequently.

Political leaders

Many political leaders all over the world employ one or multiple forms of manipulation for selfish gains. For example, we have come across leaders who downright lied or lie to the public, some twist information to give out what favors them while others use propaganda to spread falsehoods to the public as a way of influencing the public to think or behave in a certain way. Often, these tactics are used by such politicians to achieve self-serving interests.

Attorneys

Most attorneys acknowledge that winning cases is a good thing as it translates to flocking of customers which means more money. As such, most attorneys focus so much on winning that they end up resorting to using dark persuasion tactics to achieve their desired outcome. There are cases of attorneys who produced fake evidence, lied to the court and even bribed and coached witnesses to act in a certain way. All of these count as forms of deception which is a trait under dark personality.

Salespeople

This is another category of people who use manipulation to achieve desired results. To most salespeople, making a sale is the only thing that matter. Most of them do not give much thought to how what they do as long as they make a sale. Perhaps due to extreme competition and pressure from their companies, salespeople have resorted to using dark persuasion tactics to get the desired outcome. Salespeople lie out rightly, willingly twist information and deceive customers into buying their products.

Selfish people

A selfish person can be anyone as long as they harbor a selfish agenda which entails putting themselves first before others. Such people often use devious means and ways of getting what they want.

This list by no means complete as there are many people including ourselves who may at one point or another have used manipulation to get what we wanted. There are some people in society who use manipulation more than the average everyday person, for example, people listed above as well as sociopaths, sadists, and narcissists.

How can you determine if you are being manipulative?

The intention is the best determinant factor of whether a person is being manipulative or not. For example, a salesman must analyze if the tactics they are using are for their own gain or they also have the intention to genuinely help their customer. It is okay to have the intention of helping yourself in the process but it is also important to consider the other person and how they will also benefit. Your intention must have the approach of win-win for you to be considered as not being manipulative.

Some important questions that one might ask themselves as far as their motivation and persuasion tactics go include; What is to be achieved from an interaction, who is the beneficiary and how do they benefit? Have I practiced openness and honesty? Does my interaction with this person lead to long-term benefit for them? And do the tactics that I use to build my relationship with this person or destroys trust between us. If the answers you come up with are on the affirmative side, then it is likely that you are not being manipulative. If however, you evaluate yourself and your answers lie on the 'negative' side, then you are being manipulative.

The challenge of manipulation in dark personality
Understanding manipulation is quite a challenge for two critical reasons i.e. it is a wide phenomenon that permeates all dimensions of human life. Secondly, manipulation can happen knowingly or unknowingly in

the sub-conscious mind. Manipulation as an aspect of dark personality is an action that is motivated towards influencing a person's decision-making process making them act or behave in a particular manner without their direct approval.

Fused with trickery, manipulation manifests itself in infinite variations and forms using different guises from being a powerful weapon that can be used in propaganda to altruistic elements in both education and psychotherapy. Social scientists have come to a consensus that it is impossible to have an effective change in human-decision without using some form of manipulation.

It is important to understand that persuasion is not the same as manipulation. Neither is manipulation coercion neither is it similar to deception. It is an elusive phenomenon, one that most social scientists still consider having a lot of grey areas rotating between the motivating actions and the grey area itself. Because of this, there is the challenge of accurately characterizing manipulation and understanding its impact on society.

A skilled manipulator uses dark traits in a manner that both his legal and normative judgment is literally obscured. By using complex illusive strategies, a skilled manipulator is able to influence the wisdom of even the best of us. These challenges appear in every dimension of our lives from politics, relationships, education, and even intimate relationships. For example, where do we draw the line between genuine courtship between two people and sexual harassment? How can people differentiate between indecent and decent propaganda? How can we attract the attention of people to open them to innovative ideas when such people have no inclination to pay attention?

Brainwashing and dark Psychology

Is brainwashing real? While many people believe it is, a similar number believes that it isn't. Brainwashing has been made popular by movies in which a person or a group of people are depicted as being brainwashed as such cannot think for themselves but acts on the orders of their 'brainwashed'.

Psychology defines brainwashing as a way of reforming someone's thought by way of influencing them. This is one of the commonest aspects of dark psychology that is rife in our society that happens to everyone irrespective of whether they are aware of it or not. Brainwashing aims to changes core elements in humans such as our attitudes, beliefs, and behavior. For example, social scientists assert that compliance methods used in places of work can be counted as brainwashing. The reason for this is that people are required to act and behave in a certain manner when they are at their workplaces.

Further, social scientists argue that brainwashing has severe social effects than most of us realize. This is because these methods change the way we think without our approval. For example, when at work, nobody asks for your consent to follow your organization's rules and policies. You follow them as a matter of rule whether you consent to them or not. Social scientists believe that brainwashing works best when subjects go through complete isolation and dependency resulting from the invasive influence and grip on the subject.

Advertisements and marketing agencies are big users of brainwashing. In almost all TV commercials, brainwashing heavily exists. The viewer is bombarded with commercials which influence them to act or behave in a particular manner. For example, such commercials use the idea of being cool and modern to brainwash consumers. Such commercials make us believe that without such products, we are not cool enough to fit in with other 'modern people. Out of being brainwashed to believe that we are not 'cool', we allow ourselves to be influenced to change our perceptions, attitudes, and behavior to conform to the needs of the brainwasher.

Motivation and Dark Psychology

One of the motivating factors in dark psychology is manipulation. Therefore manipulation is counted as a motivating action. The fact that a manipulator does not employ a direct approach in dealing with others is evidence enough that such people are not on the same side but are people who hold contrasting positions. It has long been held that manipulation works against the interest of the people being manipulated. Judging from this, it is implicitly clear that any factor that acts as a motivator and is employed for the sole benefit of the target cannot be counted as manipulation. If however, the benefit is solely meant for the manipulator, then, one can see the element of manipulation.

Motivation makes a person to desire to move towards a certain goal. Just like you and I are motivated to go to work, look after our families or tend to our businesses, so do people with dark personality traits. The difference is that you and I do these things for the benefit of our families, friends, companions, and relatives, people with a high degree of dark personality mostly care about own interests. Again, just like you and I, people with dark personality traits also have extrinsic motivation which drives them.

In terms of deception, researchers Buller and Burgoon (1996), advanced three theories that can be used to analyze and understand motivations for deception using interpersonal deception theory. These taxonomies include; relational motivation which is employed to keep bonds strong or to maintain relationships. Instrumental motivation is employed by people with a high degree of dark to when they want to avoid being punished. Lastly, there is identity motivation which is used by people to save face or preserve their self-image.

Modes of Mind Control

There are so many ways that someone can use to control your mind or you can use to control someone's mind. Some of them have been discussed earlier in this chapter. When talking of mind control, many people's minds rush to extremes such as brainwashing. The truth is that mind control happens every day in many ways some of which we may consider mundane or inconsequential.

Most people get acquainted with manipulation when at a young age. For example, some of you may have been unfortunate enough to pass through the hands of a school-yard bully, or you may have witnessed a kid who was bullied in school. These school bullies are examples of manipulators who learned early in life the art of using intimidation to manipulate fellow students. What is sad about bullying is the finding by researchers that bullies have a pleasure response at the suffering of others. This together with the fact that such people become addicted to seeing their victims suffer because of them makes bullying one of the worst kind of dark psychology.

Mind Control Techniques

Isolation

Social scientists believe that isolation is one of the most powerful mind-control techniques known to humans. Manipulators can choose to isolate their victims using physical isolation or mental isolation. Remember your days in school as a young child. Perhaps you were one of those kids who were picked on or was never liked by fellow students because you didn't fit in. They chose to physically seclude and isolate you from their groups. This made you feel like you are less of a human being and you kept wondering what was wrong with you. In some cases, you had to do favors for your 'isolators' in order to become one of them. This is manipulation.

Criticism

Manipulators often use criticism as an isolation weapon on their victims. These people criticize everything you do and in the process make you feel that your way is inferior to their way even though you may be fully aware that this is not the case. Such people will go to great lengths to make you feel that being associated with them is a very big favor which you do not deserve in their opinion.

Peer pressure

Some people with dark traits want to influence as many people as possible to act, think, and behave as they do because they have a twisted perception that they are better than everyone thus things must be done their way or no way at all. These are the kind of people who will influence others to act and behave in a specific way because 'everyone else is doing it' and that is justification enough for them. This kind of social influence is popular with young people in schools, college, university, and neighborhoods. Peer pressure works best when an individual does not know or isn't sure how to behave, act or think.

Fear and alienation

People who are joining groups as new members often find themselves victim to this type of manipulation. They are often received warmly into these groups and even form a few friendships there. Even become surprised at how friendly these people are. Sometime down the line after making friends in these groups, you may be asked to do some things which may go against your belief or interest but since you do not want to disappoint your 'friends', you comply with their wishes. This is because you feel that the friendship is too deep to let down. You may realize when it's too late that the friendship wasn't real.

How to spot and control mind control

Zimbardo and Anderson in 1979 in their research study pointed out that having information is the best way to stop mind control. It is important for us to sieve through all the information we receive because all decisions are made based on the information that we have. Wrong and false information leads to wrong decisions. We might be made to believe that we are making our decisions freely without any influence, but that is where the danger lies.

One important thing to remember is that a manipulator thinks outside the box before they pounce on their victim. For example, it is way too easy for a manipulator to take control of your mind in situations that seem normal and then in situations where we are skeptical. In order to stop mind control and manipulation, start by analyzing the information being passed to you. Even more important, analyze how the person is communicating with you. Most importantly, do not do something just to please someone. Try to recognize the situations in which you feel vulnerable and walk away. Lastly, do not be coerced or pushed into making a decision or taking any action.

Conclusion

I wish to express my sincere gratitude to my readers who have made it to the final chapter. Your support by reading through every chapter is what gave me hope to continue writing even when I felt like quitting. The thought of letting down my fans who kept reading chapter after chapter of my book would have been too high a price for me to pay. Thank you for standing with me from start to finish.

In this book, you will be taken through what dark psychology is and how it manifests itself. Right from chapter one, you will get well-researched information about the power of persuasion and how dark psychology works in seduction. Subsequent chapters will give you in-depth information on how you can control someone's mind without their knowledge.

In chapter six, for example, you will be taken through how to use dark psychology techniques to influence the thinking of even the most charismatic person. Did you know that all of us have a dark side? You can find out more about your dark side in chapter seven. You will also learn that it is okay to use your dark side, only for good reasons and purposes. Most of us simply assume that dark personality cannot be put into good use. It is possible to harness the positive energy found in these dark traits and channel them into positivity.

It does not stop there, in Chapter eight, you will learn about advanced techniques that you can use to hack someone's mind or your mind being hacked by someone else. In chapter nine, you will get to know the techniques that people use to control other people's minds. In this chapter, you will learn about deception, isolation, criticism and peer pressure as some of the mind control techniques. You will also learn the genesis of bullying and how you can counter bullying by using mind-control techniques. You will also gain valuable information on how you can spot when you are being manipulated and put a stop to it. Chapter nine lists down the steps you can take get away from being manipulated.

This book will help you to be more self-conscious when dealing with other people. You will learn to keep your guard so that you are not easily manipulated. On the other hand, you can use the techniques you have learned in this book positively influence others for your own good and their good as well. Most importantly, you will gain skills and knowledge of choosing and determining your own destiny by making the right decisions. It is not too late to take control of your destiny. This book gives you details of what you can do to protect yourself. Now that you have the information, you can help to positively influence others around you by helping them to take control of their lives. So many dark deeds happening around the world, it is possible for one to take control of their lives by avoiding becoming a victim of manipulators.